Glory From the Ashes

How a YES to God's Invitation Can Transform Your Marriage

By: Clinton & Nikki Mitchell

Copyright © 2025 Clinton & Nikki Mitchell

Cover design and book formatting by: sarahlynnstudios.com

All rights reserved.

No part of this book may be reproduced, or stored in a retrieval system, or transmitted in any form or by any means, electronic, mechanical, photocopying, recording, or otherwise, without express written permission from the authors.

All Scripture quotations, unless otherwise indicated are taken from the ESV® Bible (The Holy Bible, English Standard Version®), copyright © 2001 by Crossway, a publishing ministry of Good News Publishers. All rights reserved.

Scripture quotations marked (NIV) are taken from the Holy Bible, New International Version®, NIV®. Copyright © 1973, 1978, 1984, 2011 by Biblica Inc.™ All rights reserved worldwide. (www.zondervan.com). The "NIV" and "New International Version" are trademarks registered in the United States Patent and Trademark Office by Biblica Inc.™

ISBN: 979-8-9929217-0-0
Do With Not For Publishing
Printed in the United States of Americ

To our family line.

We wholeheartedly embrace the difficult work of breaking generational patterns and strongholds with each of you in mind.

Especially to our own beloved children, Sarah and Luke, as well as our daughter-in-love, Sarah. You entered our lives long before we said YES to God's invitation to be transformed through Spiritual Intimacy. As you witness the fruit of our long-awaited freedom, may it draw you deeper into your personal stories of transformation with Him.

"We are born in relationship, we are wounded in relationship, and we can be healed in relationship."
~ Harville Hendrix

Praise for *Glory From the Ashes*

"Here we have a heartfelt resource that is a profound example of God's beautiful, wonderful redemption. In the pages of this book, Nikki and Clinton invite us into their lives. I was deeply touched by the Mitchells' humility, grace and tenderness that will surely encourage, edify and inspire the reader in the wonderful ways God can bring life and joy from the ashes of despair. The reflections and practices were insightful and meaningful. I thoroughly enjoyed this book. You will as well!"

~ Chris M. Coursey, President of THRIVEtoday and author of *The Joy Switch*

"*Glory from the Ashes* will raise your belief that marriages can recover from the trauma of sexual sin, even if the sin has been hidden for decades. Nikki and Clinton transparently share not only what happened, but how their journey impacted their hearts. They vulnerably let us in on details that are typically reserved for the counselor's office. You'll not only find hope but also learn about resources that can help you on your own journey to an intimate marriage."

~ Phil and Priscilla Fretwell, authors of *Savage Marriage: Triumph over Betrayal and Sexual Addiction*

"What happens when you truly say 'yes' to Jesus in your daily life? You encounter His presence like never before! Having used the tools that Clinton and Nikki teach about in their book, I can testify to the transforming power of authentically walking WITH Jesus. I have grown more in the last 6 months using these tools than I have in 20 years as a Believer. Come, taste and see that the Lord is good!"

~ Rebekah Secrest, dental hygienist and wife

"Have you ever been center stage to an unfolding miracle or wondered what a modern day, real-life example of Heaven touching earth looks and feels like? What you hold in your hands is just that. The Mitchells present their radically raw vulnerability, God's never-ending pursuit for intimate relationship, and practical tools to bridge the gap. God's work through *Glory From the Ashes* is transforming lives, marriages, and communities. This book, their story, God's glory… Are you ready to say YES?!"

~ Meredith Christy, Realtor, wife, and mother

"What a powerful story of this couple's journey to vulnerable honesty, demonstrating God's faithfulness in their healing and restoration! Their authentic testimony of the relentless grace of Jesus inviting Clinton to the place of total transparency and freedom is both riveting and inspiring! This dear couple's story is another example of how God takes the very things the enemy intends for our destruction and turns our messy broken ruins into His *Glory From the Ashes*."

~ David Kauffman, business owner, husband, father, and grandfather

CONTENTS

Forward

Preface

Part One: The Unfolding 1

Chapter One: Ground Zero 3
Chapter Two: Looking Back to Move Forward 7
Chapter Three: Is Ignorance Really Bliss? 15
Chapter Four: Choosing Unholiness 25
Chapter Five: Knowing Is a Two-Way Street 33
Chapter Six: New Take on an Old Problem 39
Chapter Seven: Lightening the Load 47
Chapter Eight: His Ways Are Higher 55
Chapter Nine: Ground Zero - The Other Side of the Coin 65

Part Two: Being Made New 71

Chapter Ten: Healing Begins 73
Chapter Eleven: Stepping Toward Forgiveness 83
Chapter Twelve: Moving at Warp Speed 91
Chapter Thirteen: A New Covenant 99
Chapter Fourteen: The Trip of a Lifetime 107
Chapter Fifteen: Intimacy - Let's Get Down to Business 117
Chapter Sixteen: What Is Spiritual Intimacy? 127
Chapter Seventeen: Living in the Light 135
Chapter Eighteen: New Every Morning 143

Acknowledgements

Notes

Additional Resources

FORWARD

The marital bond is the most profound symbol of the relationship between Jesus Christ and His church. No wonder marriages are under such attack from the Enemy of our souls. In my experience as a marriage therapist and in my own marriage of 26+ years, the marital relationship holds the most potential for deep and fulfilling human connection, as well as healing from childhood wounds. Yet, marriage is also commonly the most complicated and painful relationship most of us will ever have. One such complication involves the confusion and distortion of sexual intimacy in marriage.

Sex is a peculiar thing. Well, peculiar is one way to describe it…but it could also be described as Powerful, Beautiful, Dangerous, Exciting, Painful, Mysterious, Humiliating, Shameful, Exhilarating… and the list goes on. Could it be that sex is the most powerfully beautiful and the most dangerously painful act with which a human can engage? How is it that this one act can bring two humans into such a strong bond, create new life, bring feelings of euphoric ecstasy to the human experience, and yet be so horribly traumatizing?

God Himself warns us in the Holy Scriptures…

"Marriage should be honored by all, and the marriage bed kept pure, for God will judge the adulterer and all the sexually immoral." Hebrews 13:10 (NIV)

And…

"Flee from sexual immorality. All other sins a person commits are outside the body, but whoever sins sexually, sins against their own body. Do you not know that your bodies are temples of the Holy Spirit, who is in you, whom you have received from God? You are not your own; you were bought at a price. Therefore, honor God with your bodies." I Corinthians 6:18-20 (NIV)

As a Certified Sex Addiction and Certified EMDR therapist, I have extensive experience in treating the trauma caused by sexuality gone wrong. It is not lost on me that there is a sinister plan to destroy our sexuality before we even have a chance to experience the fullness and beautiful power of our sexual self in a positive way. Many, if not most of us, have experiences in childhood that attempt to steal the beauty of our sexuality from us. More often than not, we come into marriage full of confusion and pain in regard to our sexual self.

It is for this exact reason that Clinton and Nikki's story is so very powerful.

While both confusion and pain were a part of this couple's sexual experience at the beginning of their marriage, the story told in this book gives much hope for restoration and fulfillment. Truly, what the Enemy means for evil, God has turned into good... better than they could have dreamed or even hoped.

I love this story, and I love how God used imperfect therapists like Kyle and myself, the love of community, and most of all His own love to bring healing and restoration to Nikki and Clinton's marriage. In addition to all of this, God used the Life Model as a healing agent in this couple's marriage. Nikki and Clinton were initially introduced to the Life Model before they entered our therapy practice, but it was at our practice that they came to understand and learn to apply the Life Model to their individual lives and their marriage.

The Life Model is an idealized lifespan conceptualization based on neuroscience and biblical Christianity (also known as neurotheology). Through the Life Model, we gain perspective on what "should" have happened in each of our lives in order to have developed correctly so we can better understand what went wrong and therefore know better how to heal our malfunctions. There are three concepts that Life Model uses to promote healing for those seeking it and they are: Multigenerational Community, Immanuel Awareness and Relational Brain Skills. The therapists in our private practice in Davidson, NC (The Center for Family Transformation) apply the Life Model concepts to our personal lives and also to our treatment of individuals, couples, families and groups. We have also developed a training center (The Center for Transformation Institute) which is focused on developing Life Model Informed Therapy, a continuing education curriculum for mental health professionals, designed to provide a thorough training of the Life Model concepts in therapeutic practice.

Personally, I am thrilled to see the progress that Nikki and Clinton have made in their healing journeys, as individuals and as a couple, in such a very short amount of time. This couple is now experiencing such beauty and delight in their marriage. Their marriage is a model and inspiration to those around them, and I believe this book will help so many couples find their own healing path. Praise God that He doesn't leave us in our pain but gently guides us into full restoration and wholeness. To Him be the glory forever.

Monica Mouer, MS, LCMHCS, CSAT-S, EMDR certified
Center for Family Transformation, Founder and Director
www.familytransformation.com
Center for Transformation Institute, Founder and Director
www.cftinstitute.com

PREFACE

Our story is over three decades in the making; however, a rapid series of events shifted the trajectory of our marriage in ways we could never anticipate. Those events were a display of God's kindness, inviting us further into the narrative He intended for our marriage. Will this be an easy or comfortable story to tell? No. Do we believe you and your spouse will glean profound benefits as we share? Absolutely!

If you are like most couples, your marriage has suffered heartache at some point along the way. Ours has too, and we desire to reveal what God is teaching us on the road back. Spoiler alert: God is good, even in the devastation. *Especially* in the devastation. Our particular brand of heartache has the name Sexual Addiction, but this is not a how-to book about healing after an affair or recovering from porn use. There are plenty of wonderful resources already available on these topics. If your brand of heartache doesn't include sexual struggles, don't leave just yet.

Yes, this book tells our personal story, but it unfolds a beautiful journey to Oneness in marriage as well. Part One will walk you through the difficult challenges we faced in the first thirty years after our wedding. You may recognize similar patterns of dysfunction in your own relationship. (If they hit a little too close to home and you feel triggered, take it slowly. Use wisdom, and care for yourselves in the process. Be sure to reach out for help if you need support.) Part Two details our healing process of deeply connecting to each other and our community through shared abandon to Jesus. We refer to this as Spiritual Intimacy, and we'd like to suggest it's a vital missing piece in most relationships.

You may be wondering, what if I'm not experiencing distress in my marriage? Or what if I'm single, widowed, or divorced? Is this book for me? We believe it is! Stick with us because over and over, our testimony points to the One who transforms hearts and minds. No matter the current season or condition of your life, we *all* need to be made NEW!

If you are currently married, we encourage you to engage with this book together as a couple. The two of us have collected a myriad of exceptional tools along our journey. The majority of these aids did not originate with us, rather they were gifted *to us*. Now, we desire to pass them on to you for use in your own marriage. Discuss the concepts we introduce, then practice them with each other, *regularly*. Open yourselves to begin communicating with your spouse with honesty, openness, transparency, and vulnerability. This might feel foreign to one or both of you. It will most likely be uncomfortable, but we testify from experience, the beautiful fruit is well worth the discomfort!

Please note, if your marriage is currently in despair, you most likely didn't land in turmoil in an instant. You won't traverse the pain in an instant either. Some stories warrant professional assistance, so be open to that possibility if you bump up against things that prove too difficult to handle on your own. We are proponents of Radical Honesty, but *please* resist the urge to dump hidden secrets on your spouse without first seeking wisdom and support from trusted and seasoned advisors. At times, you may find this book difficult to read, not only because of our challenging tale, but what it may stir up in your own story. Most importantly, be kind to yourself and to each other in this tender process.

The time has come for us to take a deep breath and share our story. As you can imagine, revealing ourselves in this way requires profound vulnerability, which we gladly choose so you may experience the Lord's goodness *with* us. We pray God draws you and your spouse into greater depths of Spiritual Intimacy as you behold *Glory From the Ashes*.

Clinton & Nikki

PART ONE
THE UNFOLDING

As you read through the first half of this book, you'll notice a heavy focus on our personal history. This is intentional. We wholeheartedly believe as followers of Jesus, there is great power in sharing our testimony. And it's exactly that - *our* testimony. You may or may not relate with the details of our story; however, we encourage you to pay attention to the general areas of your marriage that we reference along the way. See if you observe similar dysfunctions, patterns of communication, various lies of the enemy, clues from your family history, etc.

While reading through the chapters, utilize the discussion questions provided and collect this valuable information as you go. Please don't skip over these activities. You may feel uncomfortable or even resistant, but we believe the Lord will reveal truth to both of you through these questions. In Part Two, we'll refer back to the discoveries about your own marital patterns and history and invite you to use them as you move toward Spiritual Intimacy with your spouse in your journey forward.

CHAPTER ONE: GROUND ZERO

Ground Zero - noun: a site of devastation, disaster, or violent attack[1]

It was May 13, 2024, a lovely day with blue skies and white puffy clouds, always a favorite. We wound along back roads and witnessed brightly colored flowers and various shades of green, both abundant in spring. I (Nikki) sat in the passenger's seat while Clinton drove, and worship music played as we traveled the 45 minutes to our therapist's office.

With eyes closed, I took several deep breaths and noticed I felt calm. I was in a really good place with Jesus. For two and a half years, I'd been in a deep dive of personal growth and healing with the Lord. Now, we shifted the work to our marriage. With our 30th wedding anniversary approaching, I was well aware of several bumps we'd experienced along the way. Our story was far from perfect; however, in the few years prior, Clinton and I made significant strides to improve communication skills and deepen our emotional connection. This therapy appointment was an opportunity to assure we were on the same page in another vital area of our relationship.

As we got closer to the office, CeCe Winans' song "Goodness of God" began to play. The beautiful chorus poured from my heart as I sang aloud to the Lord:

'Cause all my life You have been faithful
And all my life You have been so, so good
With every breath that I am able
I will sing of the goodness of God[2]

I looked over at Clinton. He was also singing, and tears ran down his cheeks. As the song continued and the bridge began to swell, he started to weep. The intensity of his emotion caused my peace to waver. This wasn't like him. What was going on inside my husband? I purposefully turned my attention back to the Lord and focused on His goodness once again. What were the words He spoke to my heart just a few weeks earlier? "Trust My Process." I uttered a silent prayer, "Alright Jesus, I choose to trust You…"

We arrived at the office and sat quietly in the waiting area for our therapist, Kyle, to call us back. A moment later, he welcomed us with his usual joyful smile, and Clinton and I walked back and settled on his couch. Kyle asked how we were feeling, and Clinton conveyed he was nervous. I echoed the same, but that I was also ready. There we sat, suspended in a moment I would only understand much later as *Holy*.

On this day, we met with Kyle to experience something called a "Full Therapeutic Disclosure." This meant Clinton was about to read a comprehensive letter, compiled in the weeks prior with Kyle's assistance, that revealed the full factual history regarding his sexual struggles. Our session would immediately be followed by a polygraph examination to confirm the truthfulness of Clinton's letter. It made sense we were both feeling nervous.

Kyle prayed for our time together, and I felt the comforting presence of the Holy Spirit in the room. Then, I shifted on the couch to face my husband. With a deep breath and trembling voice, Clinton began reading his letter to me. He started by explaining how pornography entered his life as a young teenager, and the resulting Sexual Addiction ebbed and flowed throughout our relationship. I already knew much of the information in a general sense, but putting the full timeline and new details together felt heavy. His words brought clarity to several seasons earlier in our marriage and answered why I often remembered us feeling "off." Clinton's letter recounted the ways he lied, hid his actions, and *assured* me everything was good between us in times it actually wasn't. Then, the sentence that changed everything:

"The Emotional Affair long ago was much more than I ever revealed."

My heart began to race as my body tensed. Clinton drew a deep, shaky breath, and his next words cut me to the core. It was as if he splayed me open, and my insides came spilling out onto the floor. The sentences detailing his extensive sexual affair shattered me, yet I was paralyzed. He continued to read as I sat motionless, and a single tear slid down my cheek.

Eventually, the words stopped. Clinton's letter was finished. For the remainder of our session, Kyle helped us begin processing the information, first with me alone, then with Clinton on his own. My tears bubbled up and subsided several times, but overall, I was stunned. I felt numb. Finally, the three of us came back together and made a plan for the days ahead.

The time came to leave Kyle's office and proceed to the polygraph test. I willed myself to stand and carefully gathered my broken pieces. Then, Clinton and I quietly walked to our vehicle. Once settled inside, I found the silence deafening and asked Clinton to play the worship music again. He drove 30 minutes to the location for the polygraph, and my head felt fuzzy and clouded. When we arrived, the examiner invited me back alone to discuss the procedure, and he formulated specific questions based on the information I provided from Clinton's Disclosure Letter. It all seemed like a strange dream. I couldn't think straight. After quite a while, I realized this man was still talking, and I felt desperate for him to stop. Finally, I returned to the lobby and Clinton went back with the examiner for what lasted an eternity.

As I sat alone, my muscles quivered. Initially, I chalked it up to the temperature of the room, but I began to wonder if this is what *shock* felt like. Question after question assaulted my mind. I attempted to journal my thoughts and emotions, but my brain was completely scattered. While waiting for the test to finally be over, I carefully held my emotions in check. If I allowed a single tear to fall, I feared the flood may never stop. Silently, I sat there by myself facing a difficult double bind. If Clinton passed the polygraph, it meant he was *finally* honest with me about these things for the first time in three decades. AND, if Clinton passed the polygraph, I had to face a new reality where the devastating words he spoke earlier that day were actually true.

CHAPTER TWO: LOOKING BACK TO MOVE FORWARD

"You can't go back and change the beginning, but you can start where you are and change the ending." ~ C. S. Lewis

Nothing happens overnight.

I (Clinton) didn't find myself hooked up to polygraph equipment answering questions about my sexual life "all of a sudden." It was more like the proverbial "boiling a frog" scenario. I jumped into a pot of water that didn't seem so bad at first. Over time, the temperature continued to rise until I was overcome by a perilous situation that threatened everything I held dear. Your pot might not be Sexual Addiction, but I'm sure at some point in life you've found yourself in hot water. Maybe you struggle with a different addictive behavior like overspending, drinking too much, eating for comfort, or excessive gaming. It could be much more subtle. I think we all relate with the magnetic pull to doom scroll on our phones. Have you ever been out with friends or at a family gathering, then look up and every single person is staring at their devices? Or perhaps if you're honest, you might admit you're bored in your marriage, and conversations with a coworker or friend at the gym feel a little too comfortable. At some point or another, I imagine we all end up asking the question, "How did I get here?" In order to escape the pot, I believe it's important to look back and explore how we landed there in the first place.

Before unpacking my story, I want to convey an important point of view. If you are a parent, I imagine you can relate with the fact that none of us get it *all* right. We do life in this broken world, and no matter how much we love our children, every one of us makes mistakes. It's my full intent to honor my parents as I recount events that helped shape me growing up. In no way do I blame them. As believers, we have a crafty enemy who delights in using our hardships to present lies and patterns that *we choose* to embrace, sometimes even without realizing it. Therefore, I am not telling a story of my parents' shortcomings, rather of my choices based on the lies I believed.

At 12 years old, I moved with my mom and dad to an upstairs apartment outside of Pittsburgh, Pennsylvania. It was perfectly adequate with 2 bedrooms, living room, a back den and eat-in kitchen. This new apartment wasn't the issue; the problem had more to do with my perspective.

You see, my childhood to this point encompassed the exploration of quintessential rural America, where my imagination played out on the acreage of our family farm. I grew up in a large two-story farmhouse in the beautiful Shenandoah Valley of Virginia. I remember the sprawling front porch, massive trees lining the driveway, and a one-hundred-foot pine tree in front of the house that I climbed on many occasions. There was a cottage behind the house for the well, a pumphouse, a huge barn, and garage where we kept the tractor, all surrounded by more open farmland. I rode my bike everywhere! If we journeyed through the huge cornfield on the back side of the house, there was a convenience store where we bought candy and soda. If we crossed the road in front of the house and traveled through the cornfield that way, we ended up at the North River. Growing up as a kid, all I knew was this adventurous wonderland in rural Virginia.

I was raised there in a family with 4 older siblings (all spaced about 20 months apart), then 7 years later, I arrived on the scene. My dad was a full-time minister at a local fellowship, and he traveled for some missions work overseas. Mom stayed home to tend to us kids, and she held down the fort when Dad was away ministering. The summer I was 12, the last of my 4 siblings was about to head to college. In that season of life, my brother Michael was my favorite playmate and best friend. Then, I watched as he pulled out of the driveway and disappeared from sight. Not long after that, I was plucked from my familiar school, my friends, and my beloved childhood home, and I landed in hell.

When we moved, the culture shock was intense. Everything seemed different than the slow-paced and carefree atmosphere I just left. The change screamed at me, and I felt anxious and alone. In hindsight, I recognize I was depressed, but in that season the enemy reinforced a destructive lie I already believed, "Other people struggle with those problems; we don't." You see, even as a young boy I wanted to fit in and make my parents and family proud of how I represented both Jesus and them. I needed to look and act as if I had it all together. This became second nature, and I believed since I loved Jesus and was a "good Christian," it was impossible for me to struggle with the same things as non-believers. Therefore, I didn't deal with problems or issues like anxiety or depression, because I was "victorious in Jesus." If big feelings or other challenging things surfaced, it led to the conclusion that I was NOT victorious in Jesus. This resulted in quickly dismissing what I was experiencing, because I needed to look the part. Therefore, anxiety and depression remained unnamed in me because "others struggle, I don't."

Dad was in the process of starting a new church fellowship in the area, and though my parents knew some people from previous years in ministry, I didn't know anyone. After a few weeks, it was time for my eighth-grade school year to begin. My education the year before included a private Christian school in a Mennonite community in Virginia. Now, I would face a public middle school in the outskirts of Pittsburgh. I was completely unprepared for what I was about to experience.

God blessed me with a mind that's quick and witty, but in the wrong connotation, I rapidly understood how this could lead to trouble. I was received as a smart aleck and almost immediately found myself bullied at my new school. I was regularly beat up and ridiculed which drove me even deeper into despair, because I perceived that I was all alone. The enemy seized the opportunity and offered another attractive lie, which I quickly adopted as truth, "I have to figure this out on my own." As a result, I learned how to fight and protect myself, though quite poorly at first. The combination of being bullied and this lie from the enemy reinforced the belief that I had to fend for myself. To further compound the problem, as a pre-adolescent, I naturally began isolating from my parents and others.

During my eighth-grade year, we got something I don't recall having in our home in Virginia growing up - cable tv. I remember sitting and watching the Disney Channel and MTV, not the best choice for a boy going through puberty in isolation. Television became a coping mechanism I used to avoid the stress and anxiety of life. I numbed out to music videos with girls dancing across the screen and easily escaped my feelings of culture shock and grief after moving away from home. Combine excessive snacking to the feel-good mix, and I gained about 30 pounds that school year, which didn't help the bullying issue.

Besides school, the other major part of my life centered around church. As my dad pursued growing the fellowship, I was constantly meeting new people. In the many introductions as the pastor's son, a third lie from the enemy took root that said, "I can't be wrong." Not that I couldn't be incorrect, rather I believed I couldn't be perceived as lacking. As a result, I wore a mask portraying I was "the good son" and I presented an air of utter confidence.

The stage was set, and my identity naturally reflected these lies. From the outside, I looked strong in my faith ("Other people struggle; I don't"), obedient ("I can't be wrong"), and independent ("I have to figure this out on my own"). This new identity solidified and became so real to me, because that's who I was with my parents, the folks at church, and the people at school. For decades, I never lived as *myself*. I became the me I thought people wanted to see.

Fast forward to ninth grade, we moved to a different house with a small yard and creek in the back, so I began getting outside again. I walked the 7 blocks to school each day, along with other students in the neighborhood, including a classmate from my grade. He lived about halfway between my house and the school, so we usually trekked to and from school together. Sometime that fall, we were walking home, and he mentioned a guy a few blocks away who put all his porn magazines out to the curb. He asked if I wanted to go get some before the garbage pickup took them away. Though I was curious, my false identity and lies wouldn't allow me to be seen doing such a thing. I answered no in a very judgmental way, and unphased, he went to check it out while I walked the rest of the way home by myself.

That weekend, I was drawn by intense curiosity to the spot my classmate told me about, and I could also avoid the risk of being seen by students traveling to or from school. It wouldn't seem unusual to my parents that I was away from the house on a Saturday, so I headed out. As I approached the location of the porn stash, I noticed the magazines were already gone. Due to rain damaging the stack before they were picked up, remnants of one magazine were ripped off and left behind. I bent down and picked up two damp scraps of paper, stuffing them in my pocket as quickly as possible. On the walk home, I constantly looked around to make sure no one saw what I did. I wouldn't dare take the pictures out of my pocket until I was safely at home alone.

I didn't want to risk someone finding those pornographic images in my bedroom, so I decided to hide the pages under a loose corner of carpet in the den. Occasionally, when no one was around, I carefully retrieved the two pictures and quickly became familiar with the rush of masturbation. Fear and shame wouldn't allow me to keep that porn in the house for long, but those images were burned in my mind and the hook was set.

To complicate matters in my fourteen-year-old brain, I was taking health class at school. Part of the message presented said that masturbation was a healthy way to explore your body and relieve stress. For the first time, I thought, "This is fantastic news! Apparently, I'd been feeling guilty about this for no reason!" At the very same time, deep down I knew masturbating to porn was wrong. I couldn't talk to anyone about it for fear of my image being tainted. I tried to resist, but the rush of feel-good chemicals won every time. Thus entered a highly addictive means of medicating negative emotions and stress in my life.

Living at home, I didn't have money or means to acquire more porn easily. I learned to scan my environment for everyday things that filled my eyes, like the Sears catalog or pretty girls in a rented movie. As a teenager, I formed a mental habit of objectifying women for my own pleasure, and I was completely unaware of the long-term ramifications.

Soon, I started dating and my mind was skewed by this secret addiction. Let's just say I'm not proud of my actions and how I treated some of those girls. Despite my choices, I was relieved to know I was still a virgin. Technically.

Sometime during my junior year, I experienced an "aha" moment. In our church youth group, there was a teenage couple who I noticed spoke and acted very differently when the leader was present than when he wasn't around. They wore masks to portray themselves in a better light. It dawned on me; I acted in a very similar manner. Because of the lies I believed, I still wouldn't talk to anyone about my private struggles, but I began to tighten the reins in my life. I started a prayer group in the mornings for students, and it helped with the mask I wore to look better at school. At this point, I wasn't willing to make the announcement that I struggled sexually, but I chose to make an unspoken announcement that I was better than everyone else spiritually.

Also in my junior year, I got involved in the Campus Life ministry. The meetings included kids from school as well as church, reinforcing my determination to "look the part" spiritually, across the board. The structured program and curriculum, mixed with my religious self-effort, helped curb my sexual acting out during that season. That summer, I attended the Campus Life conference with hundreds of other teenagers, and the meetings were dynamic. I experienced an excitement I hadn't felt in a long time, and the Lord extended an invitation to me for a deeper relationship with Him. I left that place wanting more of Jesus, and I had fresh hope for the future.

Your Turn:

1. Individually, take a few moments to look back on your upbringing, objectively and with kindness. Can you recognize a few influential circumstances growing up that helped shape you? We're not asking you to "get in the weeds" right now but briefly share with your spouse one difficult thing and one positive thing you recall from your childhood.

2. Do you remember a time you wore a mask in front of others? Was it to hide an aspect of yourself, portray yourself in a better light, or maybe outwardly display one emotion when deep down you were feeling something different? Share your answers with your spouse.

3. Lies are tricky little buggers. Often, we have no idea we're actually believing a lie from the enemy, because it feels like the truth. Are you aware of any lies that have influenced your life and identity? If not, are you willing to ask the Lord to reveal these things to you? Schedule some time to pray about this important topic.

CHAPTER THREE:
IS IGNORANCE REALLY BLISS?

Ignorance - noun: a lack of knowledge, understanding, or education[1]

It was the summer between my junior and senior year of high school. I (Nikki) traveled with my mom and younger brother to Virginia for a week-long Christian conference. We attended several summers prior, and I had many fond memories of my experiences. This year, something was different. Clinton would be there.

The two of us originally met four years earlier, the same summer Clinton and his parents moved to the Pittsburgh area. I grew up in Pennsylvania about two hours east of Pittsburgh, and our church fellowships gathered for a combined picnic where Clinton and I first met at twelve years old. We saw one another several times over the next few years, but at sixteen, this meeting felt different.

As my mom pulled in the parking lot for the conference, out my window I noticed Clinton walking to the dining hall. His skin was tanned and his blonde hair bleached (from his time at the Campus Life conference in Ocean City weeks before), and he escorted his mother up the front steps. My heart fluttered! What a gentleman! My mom, brother, and I got settled then joined everyone for dinner. I quickly reconnected with Clinton, and we had an easy rapport. That week encompassed wonderful times in the presence of the Lord and such fun in the youth meetings. The two of us became fast friends, and I think we both left that week feeling the possibility for something more.

The story of our dating years is for another time, but I'll briefly convey that Clinton and I lived two hours apart during our senior year of high school, so we had a long-distance relationship. We wrote letters back and forth, paid per minute to talk on the landline, and once or twice a month met halfway at a Denny's restaurant to spend time together. At sixteen, Clinton was my first boyfriend, my first kiss, and three years later he asked me to be his wife. Life was good!

Sometime before the wedding, we were talking about things we deemed important to discuss before the nuptials. I remember Clinton opening up to me and sharing he had a history with pornography and masturbation. With my extremely shy demeanor and absolutely no communication skills to engage that conversation, I felt frozen. Nobody talks about these things! Especially not "good Christian girls" like me. I thanked him for telling me, and we awkwardly moved on to the next topic. I felt distracted by his words for a moment, but quickly reassured myself, since he talked about the struggle like it was in the past. Besides, we would be married soon. If he could have sex with me anytime he wanted, surely he wouldn't be drawn to those things anymore. Right?

Six months after I graduated high school, I (Clinton) moved away from home to the town where Nikki grew up. She was already off to college in northern Pennsylvania, so our long-distance relationship continued. During this season, I worked part-time for a trash and recycling company. On my scheduled days, I arrived at work by 4am and ran behind the recycling truck for a 6 hour shift. This put me at home by late morning, and I had the rest of the day to myself. I lived in an attic apartment (which I later found out was part of a half-way house run by a local ministry), and my rent was $50 a month, utilities included. Just to give a better picture; there wasn't an overhead light in my living room, and I didn't own a lamp, so I found some Christmas lights in the eaves of the bedroom and stapled them to the ceiling as my light source. I'm talking about the large, old-school, multicolored lights. My bathroom tub was situated under the angled part of the roofline, so I jerry-rigged a sprayer from the tub spigot and this 6'2" guy precariously got a shower every day. It was definitely an adventure!

When I moved there, I served as youth minister at Nikki's church fellowship while she was away at college. Aside from work and riding my bike to visit the youth (who lived all over the county), I had lots of time on my hands. With my own money, the privacy of living alone, and no real accountability, Sexual Addiction took a front seat in my life again. This time around, I kept porn in my apartment and developed a pattern of simply giving in to temptation so I could "get on with my day." I didn't even try to fight it anymore. This created a mindset in which I didn't think I had a problem, because I wasn't spending hours a day battling against acting out, like I did when living at home.

While she was away at school, Nikki and I saw each other once a month or so. When we were together, I felt filled up by our conversations and dreaming of the future. I was relationally satisfied, therefore, porn and masturbation shifted to the back burner the weekends I was with Nikki. This naturally led me to the conclusion that when we got married, my longtime vice would finally disappear. Hope was on the horizon!

In June 1994, we got married at 19 years old. We moved hours away from family and friends so Nikki could continue college. The two of us got settled into life on our own, and my naive unspoken assumptions of married sex were quickly demolished by the freight train called *reality*. Not too long into marriage, I recognized sex wasn't living up to my hope-filled expectations. Sure, I was regularly experiencing orgasm, but something was missing. Wasn't the reward of loving God and waiting to have sex until marriage supposed to be *effortless fulfillment* in our marriage bed? How could I possibly disappoint my new wife by bringing up my dissatisfaction?

I (Nikki) also felt very confused. For all the wonderful messages of "saving yourself for marriage" and promises made by the purity culture, I quickly found married sex wasn't what I imagined it would be. Did God somehow forget I purposefully remained a virgin until my wedding night? Where was His blessing of *blissful married sex*? Our dating years were an exercise in restraint and keeping our infatuated hands off of one another. Then, we got married and things just seemed difficult in this area. Never mind the two of us didn't discuss our expectations concerning physical intimacy, before or after the wedding. Vital conversations on this topic were non-existent. I wore a well-fitting mask to convey that everything was fine with our sex life. What I didn't know at the time was Clinton wore a mask of his own, communicating the same thing. I assumed he was fulfilled, because he seemed to be enjoying himself. My lack of healthy education or example, along with complete naivety, led me to develop a false belief around sex:

Physical connection + his climax = a successful intimate experience.

The problem was, I didn't have a voice to express that I wasn't experiencing much pleasure in that equation. As a young wife, I heard the message in several of my Christian circles that it wasn't necessarily vital for me to enjoy sex, but my husband *needed it*. So, I focused on making sure Clinton was satisfied physically. Sure, I enjoyed the emotional connection; however, sex became more like a duty on the list of things I believed made me a Godly wife. Let's just say, we didn't have a great start in this area, and unhealthy mindsets quickly solidified within our first year of marriage.

We moved to North Carolina, and a new disturbing pattern emerged. It started with me discovering some sort of evidence pointing to Clinton's sexual struggles, such as a receipt for a racy movie rental or a questionable search history on the computer that he forgot to clear. Then, I sheepishly approached him about what I found, to which he responded with an "I'll do better" attitude. Finally, the two of us awkwardly packaged up the unresolved tension until the next time I found more evidence. Wash, rinse, repeat.

This cycle lacked authentic communication of how Clinton's porn use made me feel. You see, I had my own collection of lies that took root earlier in life, but mine sounded like "I'm not enough" and "I don't matter." How cunning the enemy of my soul, that he nudged me to believe those lies while I compared myself to the airbrushed actresses Clinton was viewing in pornography. I could never measure up. The despair I felt, coupled with my old familiar lies, led me to secretly use food for comfort. The resulting battle with my weight only made me feel more hopeless in this area. For a while after each porn discovery, I tried to make up for how I feared I was unattractive to Clinton by offering him more sex. Eventually, our destructive cycle started all over again.

Years into this rhythm, I vulnerably attempted to open a dialogue and asked my husband how his struggles with porn were going. This bumped up against his lie that "other people struggle, I don't" and let's just say, the conversation didn't go well. So much so, that afterwards I made a silent vow in my heart that I would immediately quit searching for evidence, stop asking about porn in general, and I would purposefully look the other way when it came to my husband's sexual struggles.

I (Clinton) assumed sex inside the context of marriage would solve all things pornography, and to be honest, I just thought it would solve *all things*. I saw Christian married sex as a miracle pill, so to speak. Therefore, when fresh temptation hit months after our wedding, it shocked me. I couldn't figure out why I was even tempted when I had the real thing. What I didn't understand then was Sexual Addiction has very little to do with sex. Rather, it's an effective way to cope with stress, avoid difficult emotions, and medicate the disappointment of unmet expectations. I wouldn't admit I experienced any of these things though, because of my old familiar lies. I was a spiritually strong Christian husband who didn't struggle with anything, thank you very much!

If you've been married for at least a few minutes, I guarantee you understand that stresses of this life inevitably come upon you. If you learned how to navigate difficult circumstances growing up, you likely possess the tools to move through such stresses. That wasn't me. Nikki and I now had two small children, a mortgage, and the responsibilities of adult life felt overwhelming. I chose to cope and medicate the hard things, and my brain already had a superhighway to relief called Porn and Masturbation. Let's be honest, my brain formed that pathway because the feel-good chemical dump *worked*. Stress disappeared, at least for a moment.

Sometime early in marriage, I encountered a Biblical principle that Moses spoke over the children of Israel in Numbers 32:23, "...and you may be sure that your sin will find you out." When I lived on my own, it was simple to keep my actions hidden from sight. Now, I had a wife who possessed a beautiful quality that I seemed to lack: attention to detail. Whether it was a receipt I neglected to throw away or words in a search bar I forgot to delete, Nikki eventually discovered my mistakes. She came to me with evidence, and I was caught. I responded with whatever I could say to *immediately* escape the conversation, the topic, and the awkward feelings. To be honest, what only fed this cycle was the fact that Nikki desperately wanted out of the uncomfortable circumstance as much as I did. There was no "dog on a bone" with her. My appeasement of "I'll do better" did the trick every time. The result? She held the proverbial rug while I swept my mess underneath, until the next time around that same mountain.

I existed in this familiar pattern for years where Nikki discovered more porn evidence, and by the amazing grace and mercy of God, He used her to bring it to my attention. I know it was Him, because it was completely out of Nikki's comfort zone to confront. As much as I desired change deep down, I still wasn't willing to humble myself and make my struggles known. So, the willpower and religious self-effort ramped back up for a while. I resisted what I truly needed, which was to surrender to Jesus in this area and be open about it with others. It complicated matters that *no one* was talking about sexual struggles - not at home, not in the church, not anywhere. I assumed that in my sphere I was the only one in this fierce and ugly battle. Thus, the cycle raged on in my isolation. Sometimes longer periods of time passed when I didn't act out physically, but the mental draw of this addiction smoldered in the background of my life. I had several different seasons of no masturbation, but behavior modification is *not* freedom.

———— •◆• ————

Here we pause in recounting the train wreck of our early patterns in marriage, but hang tight because we're just beginning to uncover the wreckage! At this point in the story, take a moment to consider: Do you and your spouse find yourselves in a less-than-healthy cycle of your own? It may have nothing to do with Sexual Addiction. Maybe it's not an addiction at all. Your pattern might include a different unwanted behavior. Perhaps your finances are a mess due to shopping your feelings away, or you face a health crisis because you're medicating with food or another substance.

Whatever you've been through or may be facing now, we want to encourage you that God lovingly approaches us with mercy and grace every time. Since He created the first humans, God's response to sin is kindness that leads to repentance. Be assured, He extends His mercy in many different ways. Sometimes, it doesn't feel much like grace or mercy. In our early days, it appeared as porn discoveries and fragile confrontations. They were God's way of saying, "I see you struggling, and I love you in the midst of it. Why don't we bring that to the Light together as you walk toward freedom in community?"

We love the beautiful truth in Psalm 145:8-9 that says, "The Lord is gracious and merciful, slow to anger and abounding in steadfast love. The Lord is good to all, and his mercy is over all that he has made."

As God patiently welcomes us with His goodness, we can respond in one of two ways. We may choose to embrace humility, laying ourselves down before Him and surrendering our will and ways. Otherwise, we choose to resist Him in pride. Our prideful response can range from simply ignoring when we sense a display of God's mercy, to a stiff-armed attitude of actively pushing Him away to continue in our sin. This is a challenging truth, but there is no middle ground here: Our only response to the Lord's tenderness to our weakness is either humility or pride. Whichever we choose, what's the result? We believe it is *more grace*. James 4:6 says, "God opposes the proud but gives grace to the humble." First, if the revealing of your sin leads you to humility, the Lord gives additional grace. Conversely, if you decide to respond in pride and continue walking in sin, He lovingly persists and circles back around to offer another helping of His beautiful mercy and grace to draw you to Himself. This pattern continues, like it did in our lives, until we *willingly surrender to God* with a humble heart. Are you ready to choose humility?

Your Turn:

1. The two of us entered our marriage with a truckload of ignorance (defined as a lack of understanding, knowledge, or education). How can you relate to this part of our story? What unspoken expectations did each of you have in the beginning of your marriage? For individual reflection: Can you identify early areas of dysfunction in how you related with one another that may still be hanging around? (Make some mental notes on this last question, and we'll revisit your thoughts in Part Two.)

2. Gently and kindly discuss what patterns you and your spouse typically follow regarding conflict. Do you patiently process through an issue until it's resolved? (If so, kudos to you! We sure didn't!) Do both of you let it fly, raising voices and talking over one another? Is one of you often quiet or checked out, while the other does most of the talking? Or do you quickly sweep things under the rug to avoid conflict all together, like we did?

3. Can you recognize a time when God extended His grace and mercy to you, even if it didn't feel good in the moment? Share your thoughts with your spouse.

GLORY FROM THE ASHES

CHAPTER FOUR: CHOOSING UNHOLINESS

*"If I ascend to heaven, You are there.
If I make my bed in Sheol, You are there."* Psalm 139:8

This chapter was by far the most difficult piece of our story to put on paper. Before moving forward, we want to take a moment to express an important caveat. Particulars are purposefully withheld from this section, including dates, lengths of time, places of employment, and other identifying details. As such, we appreciate your respectful distance as we reveal this tender portion of our journey. Imagine an intricate tapestry. The two of us stand extremely close to this piece of art. We see the individual strands of varying colors; how they all weave together and connect. This view is *ours alone* to experience. You, as our readers, are invited into our story to witness the tapestry from afar. We allow you to see the bigger picture of what all those colorful strands created. As for the details, we intend to hold them close, believing that God will continue to use this journey for our good and for His great Glory.

I (Clinton) have always been an extrovert at heart. In this particular season, I worked with a great group of people and there were a handful of us that regularly gathered together during breaks. Good conversation and easy banter existed among all of us. I loved being right in the middle of lighthearted jesting, but I wasn't afraid of transitioning into deeper, more serious discussions either. Before continuing, let me take a moment to paint a clear picture of where my homelife was during this period of my career.

I found myself in an extended season as the sole breadwinner for our family of four, as Nikki committed to stay home with our kids and manage the household. She had the mind to keenly organize our home and calendar, take care of the finances, and she "ran a tight ship." My adventurous spirit and carefree approach to life couldn't appreciate her gifts at the time. We enjoyed time together as a family, but when Nikki and I had moments alone, our conversations usually centered around what I considered the tedious aspects of life. This included important items that needed to be planned or addressed, but not completely enjoyable from my "big picture" perspective. I wanted to dream up adventures together, but it seemed Nikki's rational way of thinking only pointed out the logistical "flaws" in my big ideas.

At work, I found a welcome diversion with my coworkers. The comradery we shared provided a distraction and break from my mundane home life. We were usually all involved in the same topic of conversation, but occasionally, one specific person approached me on the sidelines, looking for advice. Sometimes this woman asked what she should do about a situation at work. Other times, she posed a question regarding a personal problem and wanted a fresh perspective. Either way, this woman valued my opinion. She listened intently to me and put my solutions to use. I became the hero. This formed a risky pattern between us, because I didn't feel like a hero at home. My coworker provided a type of fulfillment I wasn't experiencing with my wife. The connection between the two of us dangerously deepened due to the fact that she was also dissatisfied in her marriage. She desired to be rescued, and my "white knight" complex couldn't have been happier. I recognized the recipe for disaster, and I chose to turn a blind eye.

The regular affirmation I received from her was addictive. I soon found myself looking for more opportunities during the workday to come across her path, and she happily reciprocated. As with any relationship of this nature, we both adopted a "grass is greener" attitude, and our interactions at work felt fresh and exciting compared to those at home. Before long, one-on-one conversations led to inside jokes, which eventually turned to flirting and innuendos. Circumstances presented the opportunity to go into work a few minutes early or stay a little later, and we spent more and more time together privately. The two of us tip-toed on a slippery slope and quickly plummeted into the middle of an extensive Sexual Affair.

Throughout this progression, I noticed Nikki trying to connect with me more. I viewed her attempts for closeness through a distorted lens, and my reaction was to create more distance between us. She wanted to do devotions or read a self-help book together or even attend marriage seminars. It felt like the same old story: Nikki saw something "wrong" with us, then she set out to try and fix it. Many times, I appeased her suggestions to divert attention from what was actually going on in secret.

Regularly, Nikki expressed her concerns about the distance between the two of us, and especially about my "friend" from work. I convinced her there was nothing inappropriate going on, and that I was committed to her as my wife. I dispelled her doubts of my love and devotion, quickly squelching any conversations that included Nikki expressing feelings of discomfort or disappointment. I carefully crafted reasons for my longer work hours, which made perfect sense based on added duties connected to my job. Lies stacked on top of lies, and the gaslighting was prolific. My house of cards was meticulously maintained, allowing me to live two separate lives.

I (Nikki) occasionally visited Clinton at work and got to know several of his core group there. They were friendly people, and at times, different ones of us got together after hours. I made a point to show interest, asking about Clinton's day and his coworkers when he returned home. Over time, I noticed he was telling more and more stories about one certain woman in the group. At first when I brought it up, Clinton brushed my concern aside and said she was just a friend like everyone else he worked with. I tried to let it go, until something new caught my attention and the discomfort resurfaced. This time, Clinton's response was a little more emphatic. He looked me in the eyes and intently spoke of his love, affection, and commitment to me. I took a deep breath and shook the bad feelings off once again. I noticed Clinton leaving for work earlier and staying late more often. Though grateful for his commitment to provide well for us, the kids and I had less time with him, and his absence was affecting our family.

More time passed, and I expressed to Clinton that now I was feeling outright jealousy over his consistent interactions with this woman. Then, he grew defensive and said, "You have absolutely *nothing* to be jealous about. *You* are my wife." As a result, I took my concerns before the Lord. I pondered several familiar scriptures about jealousy being a sin, and since Clinton *insisted* I had nothing to worry about, I believed I needed to repent before God. This same cycle spun numerous times, and eventually, I started to feel crazy. I no longer trusted my gut. I couldn't put these words to it at the time, but I felt unsafe and tried desperately to find a measure of steadiness and security in my marriage.

Instead of focusing on what made me feel "prickly" about Clinton and his female coworker, I poured my attention into improving our marriage. I scheduled regular date nights and shared chapters of marriage books I was reading. I researched conversation starters and tried my best to dream with my husband, an extremely difficult feat for my detail-oriented mind. I even signed us up for a Christian marriage retreat, thinking a weekend away from daily responsibilities and work stress would help us reconnect. Though I centered my actions around our emotional connection, I knew our sex life was still less than what either of us hoped for. Regular and purposeful initiation of physical intimacy became my focus. I approached repair from every angle I could imagine, but the gulf between us remained. Yet, we each put on our "Happily Married" masks when around other people. Both of us operated out of lifelong lies and pride, so the masks kept people from asking questions. Looking back, I wish *someone* would have seen through our facade and been brave enough to insist we face our dysfunction.

After an extended season of these patterns, I was away for a few days and Clinton remained at home with the kids. One morning while gone, I awoke with a start from a horrible dream about Clinton and this woman being together sexually. My heart was pounding, and tears immediately began to flow. I knew Clinton would already be at work, but I needed some comfort. Still shaking, I called him and shared the disturbing details of my nightmare. Clinton helped me calm down and provided reassurance that it was just a bad dream. We finished our conversation, and I got ready for my day; however, I couldn't shake the horrible images that startled me awake that morning.

A week later, I witnessed a specific set of circumstances at Clinton's place of employment that sent my mind and heart in a tailspin. It was *obvious* he and this woman were way too comfortable around each other. For two days after that, I felt rattled and confused. The only thing I knew to do was pour my heart out before the Lord. I shared how it affected me to see Clinton and this woman together. As I wept, I told Jesus how I was trying to improve my marriage, but it didn't seem to be working. I asked Him what I should do, and then I got quiet and listened. After a moment, I heard His familiar comforting voice say, "Look at the phone records." What?? I resisted, reasoning that the thoughts were just my jealous musings returning. Then, I heard His voice again, "Go to the computer, and pull up the phone records." This time, I obeyed. As the virtual documents loaded, my stomach sank. The section of our cell phone bill for Clinton's line listed call after call, text after text, back and forth between him and this woman. Because she and I were acquaintances, I had her cell number, so there was no doubt it was Clinton's coworker. My suspicions were true. They were involved in an Emotional Affair. Now, I had to determine what to do.

I printed out the phone records for the previous four months, which was the extent of the history available online at the time. Then, I took a highlighter and noted every call and text between the two of them. I made a copy for Clinton and one for myself. That evening, I planned to approach him once the kids were asleep in bed. My stomach was in knots all day. The opportune moment came, and I asked Clinton to sit before me on the couch. I couldn't think of another way to open the conversation except to apologize for my part in driving him away to be emotionally entangled with another woman. Tears welled in my eyes as I handed him a copy of the phone records. He looked through the pages of highlighted proof as I sat quietly. After what felt like an eternity, he looked up and said he had no idea they had been talking that much. He acknowledged it was inappropriate and immediately asked me to forgive him. I was extremely hurt and not sure I could move through this important task so swiftly, but if I hesitated or asked for more time, I feared my husband could leave me for *her*. In that fragile moment, I chose forgiveness, mostly out of anxiety for my future.

We briefly discussed what would happen the next day. Clinton agreed to take the phone records to work and let this woman know he couldn't continue in their familiarity, jeopardizing his marriage. Before concluding our conversation, he looked tenderly in my eyes and spoke of his love for me, as well as his commitment to us. We finished, then got ready for bed in awkward silence.

The next morning as I (Clinton) drove to work, my mind buzzed over the events from the night before. When Nikki handed me the highlighted phone records, I panicked. Then, I quickly regained my composure as I replayed her words from the moments before. She *assumed* my involvement with this woman was simply an emotional one. Though this relationship was in fact emotional, I now had an "out" for my sexual indiscretions, and I gladly took it. I chose to let Nikki continue to believe there was no physical contact with my coworker. Nonetheless, she seemed genuinely hurt over what she accepted as truth, and I didn't like seeing her that way. I wasn't looking forward to breaking things off with the other woman either, but there was no option. My wife was now on high alert, and I wouldn't be able to hide in plain sight anymore. On one hand, I felt extremely relieved to be found out. My double life was taking a toll. I could barely recognize myself anymore. On the other hand, my soul was entangled with the other woman and our encounters served as medication, soothing the dissatisfaction in my life. I was in a tough position. The agony I just caused my wife would only be complicated by the pain I was about to inflict on my affair partner. To make matters worse, the consequence of sin committed against myself was amplified as I perceived a great distance from my Savior. Immediately, I began a pseudo walk of humility, and I committed to repairing my marriage. At the very same time, I made an oath that day. I vowed to *never* speak of the sexual nature of my extended affair, unless God literally forced my hand. This secret would go with me to the grave.

I (Nikki) felt anxious as I waited for Clinton to return from work that day. He arrived at normal time, not late as was his custom for many months. I got the kids settled with a short video, then Clinton and I walked outside to talk. He recounted how things went, and said his coworker cried and she went home early. Clinton talked about how that made him emotional, because he was the source of her pain. This stung deeply for me to hear. I recognized no emotional reaction from Clinton the night before when *I* was shedding tears over *my* deep hurt. I wasn't able to communicate that to Clinton, but I felt some hope that he was willing to move on and reconcile with me. I suggested we meet with a particular pastor and his wife to make sure we did things right. He agreed and a few days later we began meeting weekly as we repaired what I knew was broken, our emotional connection. After all, that's what Clinton sought out with the other woman, right? For many months, the four of us met and worked through a book together regarding Emotional Affairs. Friendship slowly improved between the two of us. Clinton and I worked really hard, purposefully dating and practicing better communication with each other. It was a slow road with bumps along the way, but over time I fully believed our marriage was stronger for traversing this difficult season together.

Your Turn:

1. In our early years, we didn't know how to dream with one another. One of us was a "big picture person," the other could easily get lost in the details, and it was a source of contention between us. Can you relate? If so, who is the dreamer, and who is the realist? Choose a lighthearted topic to practice dreaming about together. Set a timer for 10 minutes and discuss your dreaminess with no concern of decisions or expectations. Just have some fun here!

2. When stress begins to mount, what do you turn to for relief? Sugary treats, caffeine, social media scrolling, binging your favorite show, or maybe there's something more serious that you need to face? Exercise mutual kindness as you discuss some of your own personal stress relievers with your spouse.

3. Song of Songs 2:15 says, "Catch the foxes for us, the little foxes that spoil the vineyards, for our vineyards are in blossom." It is vital that we're on the lookout for "little foxes" that try to come between us and our spouse. If we don't pay attention, they can easily grow into things that destroy our marriage. Take some time separately to consider: What foxes do we need to catch *now* to keep our vineyard safe? (We'll revisit your discoveries in Part Two.)

CHAPTER FIVE:
KNOWING IS A TWO-WAY STREET

"...and knowing is half the battle." ~ G.I. Joe

Fast forward many years. In January 2022, I (Nikki) embarked on a new therapy journey and the Lord uncovered several lies hidden deep in my mind, replacing them with His beautiful truth. He tenderly healed many wounds from my past, and as the months went on, I grew closer and closer to my loving Heavenly Father. The details of this precious time are mine to treasure, but I will tell you, I felt nearer to God than in any other season of my life to that point.

Though I attended therapy sessions on my own, I shared all my experiences with Clinton as they occurred. We were best friends and empty-nesters now, and I wanted him to know me better as I finally unearthed *the real me*. I recounted my sessions with EMDR, a therapy technique used to deal with negative feelings and reprocess traumatic life events. Clinton was amazed at how I was changing, healing, and growing. He supported me and was with me through it all.

That summer, I sensed a new invitation from the Lord. His lovely familiar voice whispered, "Are you ready to go even deeper with Me? I have freedom and healing available in your sexual relationship with your husband as well. Are you willing?" My heart was already poised toward Him, and I surrendered with a smile. "YES, Lord. I want the *best* of what You have for me, in all the areas of my life."

I immediately understood what God's invitation meant. It was time for me to be completely open and honest with Clinton. I needed to share that to that point (28 years into our marriage), climax wasn't a part of my sexual experience with him. In no way did this mean I was faking orgasm. There was a much larger story at play involving the enemy's lies in my heart and mind. I didn't look forward to revealing the truth regarding my lack of sexual fulfillment to Clinton; however, I knew God required my honesty if the two of us were going to move toward healthy and mutually satisfying physical intimacy as He intended.

It's important to describe the longtime dynamic of my inner world leading up to this moment. Looking back over the many years when I was ignoring the presence of Clinton's sexual struggles, I remember researching everything I could about improving sex in the context of a Christian marriage. I devoured information! I got my hands on every book I could find on the subject, 26 to be exact. The problem was not every marriage book written from a Biblical perspective did a good job teaching on the topic of sex. An even bigger problem was I had no idea that was the case. I believed and tried to incorporate the concepts I was reading about, and unfortunately, many reinforced my already unhealthy patterns with my husband. Several old familiar lies reverberated in me, "I'm not important. I don't matter." This deception led to a codependent lifestyle between me and the people closest to me. I operated from the false idea that if everyone else was happy, I was happy. *Their* needs mattered, mine didn't. This directly affected my sex life in a destructive manner. As long as Clinton was sexually satisfied, I would be fine. I could do without. But somewhere deep inside, I wanted better for my marriage. Occasionally, I read chapters of these books aloud to Clinton, but transparent dialogue about sex was still missing between the two of us. Throughout those many years, I found myself in a loop of longing for more in our sexual experiences, trying desperately to figure out how I could be different, then feeling way too vulnerable and closing off again. I resigned and thought, "Never mind. Things aren't really that bad," and eventually the cycle began all over again. Of course, I wasn't communicating any part of this loop to Clinton, or anyone else. For many years, I silently carried the burden of this dysfunction in our relationship and tried to solve all our sexual problems on my own. I didn't understand that overlooking the Lord's beautiful design for *mutuality* in marriage, my efforts were futile without my husband's loving participation.

After answering YES to God's invitation the summer of 2022, I stepped out on a limb and asked Clinton if he would consider going to sex therapy with me. I was so pleased when he agreed. Because I was the one struggling with fulfillment, I assumed our focus would be to "fix" me. Besides, I wholeheartedly believed *I* was the one broken in this area. I found a Christian woman online who was a Certified Sex Therapist with a Biblical lens. Clinton and I soon embarked on an extremely vulnerable and challenging season together.

In the first virtual session with our sex therapist, I (Clinton) was shocked when Nikki communicated that she didn't experience climax when we were together. Not that it just wasn't happening sometimes, but it wasn't happening - period. Twenty-eight years?? How could I not know this? I was stunned.

This new information immediately led me to a troubling conclusion: *I was inadequate.* What did it say about me as a man, a husband, a lover that I hadn't satisfied my wife in 28 years of marriage?? In the moment of hearing Nikki's vulnerable openness about her lack of sexual fulfillment, all I received was the negative message it portrayed about *me*. Reality was, my early years with pornography taught me to be a selfish lover. I learned to focus on my own pleasure and fulfillment in our marriage bed, and just assumed my wife would do the same. Needless to say, I chose to hide my pain regarding Nikki's honesty. I walked a precarious line between desiring to be fully known by my wife and refusing that same knowing, because it would require my past sexual transgressions coming to light.

Nikki and I moved through months of therapy exercises and homework, including extensive conversations about the deeper issues in our relationship. Our emotional connection strengthened even more, and it was fulfilling for both of us. During this season, our therapist asked us to agree on a period of abstinence from intercourse so we could break out of old patterns and learn new pathways together. I was completely committed to the process with my wife, and grateful to the Lord for sobriety from any sexual acting out during our therapy journey.

Throughout this season, I (Nikki) worked diligently to stay completely open and transparent with Clinton. I purposefully shared my deepest thoughts and feelings as we walked that challenging road. Sometimes, it took an extremely long time for me to formulate words and finally say them out loud, but my husband was so patient and kind. Not an easy journey, but it felt amazing to be seen, heard, and known in this way for the first time in my life!

Eventually, we "reached our goal." Though we still had to practice connecting and loving each other from our new healthy mindsets, sex was finally working for both of us. I shared *all* of myself with Clinton. He knew me, and I knew him.

Or so I thought...

You see, at that point in our lives, we completely missed the mark in what it means to be fully known. We believed a false assumption that simply opening yourself up to your spouse automatically results in them knowing you. If one spouse in the relationship is still withholding vital pieces of themselves (or as in our case lying and keeping secrets), the knowing remains inauthentic. Any form of intimacy, whether emotional, spiritual, or even physical, can never exist if it's one-sided. You may be familiar with the portrayal of intimacy as "into-me-you-see." When one person in the marriage is refusing to reveal, refusing to allow themselves to be truly seen, intimacy is *not actually present*. More to come on the concept of knowing and being known, but for now, are you open to cracking the door on this essential practice with your spouse?

Your turn:

1. The two of us went around the same mountain for decades in our sexual relationship. Finally, we chose to seek a professional who could assist us with getting out of our old familiar patterns. Is there an area of your personal life or your marriage where you're feeling stuck? If so, are you willing to consider getting some outside help? Discuss one step you could take to move in that direction.

2. When Clinton heard my struggles with sexual fulfillment, he immediately received it as a reflection of *his* inadequacy. When your spouse is open about a difficulty in their life, do you tend to take it personally? Brainstorm with your mate on ways you might receive one another's vulnerability objectively.

3. Have you gotten to a place in your relationship where you believe you fully know your spouse, and likewise, they know you? Are you open to the idea that there is *always* more to learn and discover about one another? How does that make you feel?

GLORY FROM THE ASHES

CHAPTER SIX:
NEW TAKE ON AN OLD PROBLEM

"What has been is what will be, and what has been done is what will be done, and there is nothing new under the sun." Ecclesiastes 1:9

In January 2023, the fine woodworking business we started together in 2012 began to explode. MitchellCraft was focused on high end custom cabinetry. We grew exponentially, adding digital systems as well as several crews, and our calendar was full! As the cash flow increased, so did the stress. By spring, our bodies began to pay the price. We consistently put in 60-80 hours a week and the phone continued to ring with more work. We encountered multiple challenging projects and clients in a row, and something had to give. Mid-July that year, we planned to take a week off to regroup. Through a series of events too long for this story's telling, God got our attention and revealed it was time for a change. A big change. That week, we prayerfully decided to restructure our business and downsize to building only custom wooden furniture. Relief was in sight, but old ways had already reemerged…

In that season drenched with stress, I (Nikki) noticed a difficult pattern developing between us. I worked long hours managing our business while Clinton spent his days engulfed in the physical and mental labor portion. We only had a few hours each evening together, and frankly, I missed my husband. Clinton came home completely exhausted, and though I desperately wanted to connect and spend time together, I gave him space to relax and unwind. Our evenings encompassed binging Netflix together, or Clinton zoning out on his iPad while I sat beside him, scrolling on my phone and feeling lonely. The transition out of cabinetry work couldn't come fast enough for me!

Late September 2023, Clinton was hard at work in the shop one day, and I needed to retrieve a business contact from his iPad. I quickly found the information, then by habit, started clearing out all the open apps. As I moved through them, one particular app caught my attention. It was unfamiliar, so I opened it. My stomach sank as I discovered recent pornography on my husband's iPad. Immediately, I closed the app and put his device away. I panicked and began pacing around the house. How could this be? We worked so hard in sex therapy, and I thought we were finally good in this area! How could this be happening again?

It would be hours before Clinton finished for the day, which was good, because I needed time to figure out what to do with this discovery. After almost two years in therapy, with the Lord healing me and revealing more of my true identity, I couldn't just turn a blind eye. I was a very different woman than when I found porn in the early years of our marriage. There would be no sweeping it under the rug! This time, I would face it head on.

When Clinton finally returned from working, he headed for a shower while I focused on staying calm, with the Lord's help. Clinton finished and came to the great room to put his feet up. I sat near him and said I needed to talk about something. With a deep breath, I recounted how and what I discovered on his iPad that afternoon. I steadily kept eye contact and waited for his response. With a look of resignation and a sigh, he told me he'd been struggling with porn for several months. It was difficult for me to remain present as my mind raced through our recent calendar. I knew Clinton was stressed and overworked, but I had no idea the extensive time spent on his devices involved behaviors I assumed he'd stopped long ago. With a quiver in my voice, I shared how his choices made me feel as a woman. How could I possibly compare to what he was viewing? My husband assured me it wasn't like that, but I didn't know what to believe. He explained the progression. First, something mildly suggestive caught his attention. Then, he began to linger and look for more. Before long, he was back to searching for explicit pornography. Clinton gently took my hand and spoke of his love for me, then said he wanted to take a break from all his devices for a while. I agreed that was a wise decision, and we tentatively went on with our evening. Later in bed, sleep eluded me as my mind raced with a myriad of anxious questions.

The next day, I found my thoughts slipping to old well-worn pathways. "Maybe I'm just not alluring enough for Clinton. How could I spice things up for us? Maybe if I initiated sex more often, he wouldn't have to turn to that stuff in the first place?" I sensed old pressures returning, like I was somehow responsible for keeping my husband satisfied in bed, and therefore, safe from porn. My mind traveled down an unhealthy path, and I didn't like where it was going. I just spent almost two years working really hard to uncover my true identity with Jesus, and at a moment's notice, I was willing to ignore my authentic self to keep my husband from looking at other women?? No. I couldn't do it. That afternoon, I reached out to our sex therapist and made an appointment for the next day.

She knew pornography and masturbation were a part of Clinton's past from our initial therapy intake sessions. With kindness, she shared that these types of coping mechanisms are highly addictive due to the feel-good brain chemicals being released. Also, these behaviors don't just "go away." She supposed Clinton probably had periods of sobriety throughout his life, but in times of stress, his brain remembered an effective way to feel better. In the current season of extreme work stress and exhaustion, it made sense pornography resurfaced. She assured me Sexual Addiction is not actually about sex, rather avoiding or medicating emotional pain. I bristled at that term: *Sexual Addiction*. What did that even mean? Clinton loved the Lord. He spent his entire life ministering to and encouraging others in Jesus. He had a great family and his own successful business. He was committed to me, and we were approaching 30 years of marriage! Now, I had to face the fact that he might have an addiction?? I felt confused and alone.

By the end of the session, my therapist scheduled another appointment with me and Clinton to create a plan for moving forward in health and recovery for both of us. A week later, the three of us met as Clinton and I learned about something called a Disclosure Letter. This was a document Clinton would write detailing his history with sexual struggles throughout his life. Then, he would go over it with our therapist on his own. During the following appointment, he would read the letter aloud to me so the three of us could process it together. In the weeks Clinton was preparing, I had the opportunity to provide him with specific questions I'd like addressed in his letter. I jotted down a few things I was curious about, but mostly I wanted assurance that there was no physical contact during the Emotional Affair long ago. It would feel good to finally have complete closure on that difficult chapter of our lives.

The day I (Clinton) was found out and Nikki discovered my recent porn use, I landed in a quandary. I desperately wanted freedom from my lifelong sexual struggle but couldn't comprehend why God wouldn't just take it from me. How many times would I traverse this particular mountain in my life? Didn't He want me to be free? I prayed. I meditated on scripture. I asked God to heal me, but this old familiar war had resurfaced in my life yet again. I believed the Lord was able, but I didn't understand why He didn't seem willing? Weariness and frustration prevailed; however, I still wasn't ready to expose the whole truth. I asked God to free me from my sexual strongholds, but I didn't realize He was actually inviting me into a journey to freedom that encompassed *all of me*.

After her personal therapy season beginning in 2022, Nikki was a very different woman than ever before in our relationship. That afternoon, she approached the discovery of my porn use with a quiet confidence that took me off guard. I offered vague information regarding the pornography on my iPad, tried to reassure Nikki of my love and commitment, and said I would make changes. This was *way more* than I gave in our early encounters, and I anticipated our usual dance of cooperating to get this thing back under the rug where it belonged. The next day, I heard my wife would meet with our sex therapist about the porn discovery, and for the first time in our marriage, we weren't going to deal with the problem "in house." More than just the two of us would know about the situation, and this was *not* our usual M.O.

  I soon realized I was expected to write a letter listing all my various periods of struggle with sexual sin, and my mind raced toward damage control. How little could I share and still be seen as honest and forthcoming? What could I say to tie this thing up with a bow, satisfying our therapist, and especially my wife? Then, I received a list of items Nikki wanted addressed in my letter, and things ramped up. She asked specific questions about the extent of the Emotional Affair long ago, and I made a decision to lie and say pornography and masturbation "kept me safe" from any physical contact with this woman. I was unwilling for the truth to come to light. So, I formulated a letter that reflected the version of the story Nikki believed all along concerning that relationship. It worked to my favor that we met with our therapist virtually. She was on a screen, we were on a screen, and I didn't have to feel the full gravity of an in-person experience. I read the letter, and both the therapist and Nikki seemed appeased. Therefore, I believed we would move on from this whole uncomfortable topic for good.

  I didn't anticipate Nikki joining a support group for wives of sex addicts to learn more about what *we* were going through. I also didn't anticipate her suggesting I find a group of men to be accountable with in order to turn away from my lifelong struggles. For a month or so, I "paid my dues" by listening to Podcasts or audiobooks on the subject of Sexual Addiction, hoping that would satisfy my wife's expectations of me. She gently and consistently inquired if I found a group to get involved with yet. I was holding out for an online accountability group that preserved my desire for anonymity and provided a place I wouldn't have to feel so exposed. After a few more weeks, and several slip-ups with Nikki finding suggestive reels on my devices, the day finally came. On a Tuesday afternoon in early November 2023, my wife handed me a piece of paper. She said, "I found a Pure Desire group[1] that meets tonight at this church fellowship. Here's the address. You're going." I wasn't happy, but I knew the shell game I'd been playing just came to an abrupt end. Now, I'd be required to sit across the table from other men and face this part of my story for the first time ever.

The first few weeks, I (Nikki) could tell Clinton wasn't sure about the group. He did the homework and expressed he was surprised at how authentic these guys were about their struggles, but I could sense he was hesitant about revealing his own life. His Disclosure Letter in late October gave me insight on how pornography entered his world at age 13 and that it continued to pop up at various times throughout our marriage. Clinton assured me there was no physical contact during the Emotional Affair, and I felt relieved to finally lay those old nagging questions to rest for good.

In November and December that year, I prayed fervently for my husband. I knew his mind was resistant to opening up, and his heart was far from Jesus. As the days passed, my prayers grew desperate. "Lord, bring Clinton to his knees. Please, let my husband fall on the Rock and be broken. Help him face his story head-on with You, the gentle Healer. And God, if he's not willing to humble himself and be broken, I ask You to crush him, for his good and for Your Glory. Please, *please* protect my heart in the process, Jesus." I was grateful for my "Betrayal and Beyond" support group,[2] a tribe of women who understood what I was going through, where I could openly express my wide range of emotions. None of our friends or family knew what I was going through at the time, so my support group provided a safe place to be authentic about this difficult aspect of my marriage.

We navigated the holidays that year and on January 2, 2024, Clinton came home from his Pure Desire group with a fresh revelation from the Lord. I couldn't remember the last time he shared something he heard from Jesus, so I felt excited to listen. Clinton recounted the ride to his group and how he heard the Lord say, "The same way you intentionally repaired with Nikki after the affair, I want you to repair with Me." My heart sprang to life as I imagined my husband finally reconnecting with Jesus! With a smile, I asked, "How did it feel to hear Him say that?" Without any hesitation, Clinton answered, "It sucked." His answer surprised me with a visceral reaction. I couldn't understand his response, so I asked, "Why's that?" He flatly replied, "It means I have to get up off my ass and do something about it."

In the days that followed, my prayers for Clinton ramped up. In moments between daily tasks, I uttered fervent prayers for the man I loved. I worshipped, I journaled, I took Clinton before the Father. Then, two weeks later, I discovered more revealing photos on Clinton's iPad. I felt angry and deeply hurt. When he came in from work, I asked him to sit on the loveseat in our bedroom with me. I opened his iPad to the questionable images, showed him, and firmly asked, "*What is this??*" He was silent. No defense, no rebuttal. I did my best to respect the man in front of me while explaining how this would *never* be okay with me. Hot tears slid down my cheeks and after a quiet moment I asked, "Have you been repairing with Jesus yet?" He said no, and I continued, "When do you think you'll start?" My husband looked at me with a blank stare and said, "I don't know." I told him that was valuable information, and I quietly stood up to leave for my support group that evening.

As I drove the 40 minutes to my meeting, tears continued to flow freely. Questions and fears bombarded my mind. Did Clinton even *care* how his actions made me feel? What if he continued to resist surrendering to the Lord in this area? Would he ever repair his relationship with Jesus? Divorce didn't cross my mind; however, we were no longer Spiritually compatible. I had to face a grim reality concerning my marriage that night: I may have to move on in my walk with Jesus by myself.

Your Turn:

1. Separately, take a 30,000 foot perspective of your marriage, and determine what unhealthy patterns you recognize that continue to surface over and over again. Choose one of those patterns to bring up with your spouse at a time you are both feeling calm and connected. Approach your spouse gently by asking, "Would you be open to praying with me about our pattern of…?" If so, plan a time to pray together. If your spouse is not willing to do that yet, bring your concerns before Jesus for now.

2. Take a few moments to talk about the upcoming week. Can you recognize anything that is potentially stressful for one or both of you? In what ways can you actively support one another as you approach those things this week, instead of relying on coping mechanisms to deal with the stress?

3. Think about ways you are on the same page as your spouse, spiritually speaking. Take turns expressing your gratitude aloud with one another. (For example, "I'm so grateful that we both value the importance of connecting with other believers on a regular basis." Or, "I'm really thankful that you take time with me every day to pray over our children before they go to sleep.")

CHAPTER SEVEN: LIGHTENING THE LOAD

"I've carried a burden for too long on my own
I wasn't created to bear it alone
I hear Your invitation to let it all go
I see it now, I'm laying it down, I know that I need You"
~ Lyrics from Matt Maher's song "Run to the Father"[1]

    The evening I (Nikki) drove to my support group feeling alone and spiritually isolated, God showered His love and affection over me in an unmistakable way. Her name was Monica. Monica owned a therapy practice in the area, and that night, she was the special speaker at my "Betrayal and Beyond" support meeting. She was something called a CSAT (Certified Sex Addiction Therapist), along with several others at her office. A young woman named Jessica attended this meeting with her, as she was training to become a CSAT. The concepts Monica and Jessica shared echoed specific principles, including experiencing joy and *hesed* in the context of healthy community, that I learned a few months prior from a book called *The Other Half of Church*.[2] I was intrigued and felt a spark of hope inside. After the meeting, I connected with Monica and asked several questions about my interaction with Clinton just a few hours earlier. I sensed the Holy Spirit in her answers, and I knew it wasn't a coincidence God brought her across my path that very night. Monica invited me to consider joining several other women at her office for something she led called a Women's Identity Group, but more on that later.

For days after our exchange in mid-January, tensions were high between Clinton and me. We communicated very little, only speaking what was absolutely necessary. There were no warm embraces, no kind words of affection, and my husband's eyes didn't *twinkle* at me like they normally did. We were two separate people existing under one roof. We slept in the same bed, but there were miles between us. I waited patiently for the Lord to soften my husband, while holding on to the hope Monica instilled a few nights prior. I respectfully gave Clinton space to process. For now, all I could do was pray, so that's exactly what I did.

The night after the confrontation about my walk with Jesus, I (Clinton) attended my weekly Pure Desire group as usual. Honestly, it felt good to be out of the house for a bit. At home, I couldn't get away from my feelings of Nikki's unmet expectations. I was frustrated and needed a break. That night, God offered me a gift I had no idea I needed. His name was Pete. I already knew Pete, a 69-year-old man who was a mentor over the guys in my Pure Desire group, but this night something shifted. During the meeting, I was distant and spoke very little, which was out of character for me. Pete must have noticed. Afterwards, he approached me, and I opened up about Nikki's confrontation the day before. I hashed out my thoughts and feelings with Pete, and he listened with kindness. He didn't correct me or offer advice. Pete loved me right where I was, right in the middle of my mess. He saw past my sin to the *real me*, and it broke something inside. I caught a glimpse of how my Heavenly Father saw me, through Pete's eyes, and I would never be the same.

For days after that, I found myself in a war. My spirit longed for truth and freedom, but my soul desired escape and comfort. Two distinct parts of me were in direct opposition to each other. The battle raged all week, and I felt like I was losing my mind. I held distance from Nikki, and I hyperfocused on work to pass the days. The following Tuesday, I showed up early for my Pure Desire meeting to connect with Pete again. His smile of acceptance brought a measure of peace to my weary heart. During that meeting, one of the men shared a scripture he heard on the "Daily Audio Bible" app[3] and afterwards, I asked him to share the app with me.

The next morning, a passage of scripture came to my mind from Ephesians 5 about being cleansed by the washing of the Word.[4] Reading remained a difficulty for me due to dyslexia, so the "Daily Audio Bible" app seemed a helpful option to consume the Word. It was January 24th, but I played the reading for January 1st. As I got ready for work, I listened to the words from Genesis, then a Psalm and a Proverb. When it was over, I played the reading for January 2nd. Then, January 3rd. For several days, I binged this audio Bible. It helped me feel sane during the fierce battle with my thoughts. I finally began to feel steady, until a new obstacle presented itself.

Nikki noticed me listening to the Bible, and she started sitting with me in the mornings as it played. Let me say, her motivations were pure. She probably felt the tiniest bit of safety as I inched my way toward Jesus, but I was still closed off. I don't blame her for wanting to connect with me spiritually, but *I* needed this time in the Word. This was my rescue vehicle, and it seemed like she wanted to hitch a ride. It reminded me of our old patterns of relating. All I could see were Nikki's spiritual expectations of me, even though I'm sure they weren't really there. I was just in a very fragile state of cracking the door of my heart to Jesus again.

Late January 2024, I agreed to see Kyle, another CSAT at Monica's therapy practice. Between the sessions with Kyle and my weekly support group, I was softening toward the Lord and slowly opening up to other men. I took my Pure Desire homework more seriously. Around that time, we had a lesson diving into the ten most painful events in our lives. For each of the ten, we were asked to consider the following questions:

1. What part of the pain am I responsible for? What part do I need to let go?
2. How did this affect the most important people in my life?
3. How has this event affected life for me today?[5]

I wasn't accustomed to paying attention to my feelings, and as they rose to the surface during this exercise, it exhausted me. Nikki inquired how my homework lessons were going, and I told her it had been tough uncovering these ten painful memories. She asked if I was open to sharing them with her, and though I really wasn't ready yet, I offered a few of the less painful items from my list. Over the course of the following weeks, she gently asked if I was willing to share more. Eventually, she heard the whole list. While her pursuit was intended as a bid to know me more deeply, I couldn't see it that way at the time. Her request to come close and experience more of me was received as a warrant, demanding access to things I didn't want to reveal. In these interactions, I couldn't see Nikki loving me for *me*. It felt more like she was loving me for opening up to her about things that made her feel safe; for her own benefit and not my ultimate healing. As a result, I still held some distance between us.

In early March, a small piece of paper showed up on our refrigerator. Apparently, Nikki heard a concept on a Pure Desire Podcast[6] and placed it on the fridge without a word. Her note read, "We can only be as free as we are willing to be honest." My stomach dropped as I took in the words. At this point in my journey, I desperately wanted to be free, but I still wasn't willing to be completely honest. I never spoke of my difficult double bind, though that little square of paper stared me in the eyes on a regular basis.

In this season, I poured my attention into building community with several men from my group. Pete continued to be a source of great encouragement, acceptance, and life for me as well. The two of us spoke during weekly calls and met for lunch regularly. I opened up to Pete about my reconnection with the Lord and shared things the Holy Spirit was revealing to me. God had begun speaking to me about being the spiritual head of my home for the first time in my marriage. The Lord laid out some practical ways I could cover my wife while living under *His* perfect covering. Pete heard and received the revelations I shared, without an ounce of judgement for the man I once was. This brand-new experience felt incredibly fulfilling.

Pete and the other men in my Pure Desire group heard me talk about my history with pornography and masturbation, as well as the "Emotional Affair," but no one knew about the extensive sexual nature of that affair. *No one.* I still planned to keep that locked away, even though it felt so good to be known and accepted by other men in my life. What would happen if Pete knew the whole truth? I couldn't risk jeopardizing what this man had become to me. So, I kept my dark secret locked away in the vault of my heart.

As things steadily improved for Clinton in early 2024, I (Nikki) got involved with one of Monica's Identity Groups. The seven other ladies were well established, and I joined the mix a few weeks into their spring semester. In the introductions at my first meeting, I felt strangely drawn to one woman in particular. I had no idea why, so I carefully shifted the feeling to the back burner. This Identity Group was now made up of eight of us who loved Jesus, wanted to grow and mature in our relationship with Him and others, and supported one another without reservation. Every two weeks we gathered to open our lives with each other, both burdens and blessings alike. This was a safe place where we could talk about "all the things." I learned how to share and cultivate joy with these women, and Monica taught us how we could return to joy after experiencing difficult emotions.[7] The eight of us also had a text thread that served as a regular connection point to ask for prayer, share our wins in life, and offer encouragement or cheer one another on in challenging times. In the beginning, I knew a limited amount about these women, but God faithfully wove our hearts together in a supernatural way.

Early April 2024, the eight of us traveled to the North Carolina mountains for a weekend retreat. There was something very bonding about enjoying meals together and having relaxed time to talk and get to know one another better. During the course of the weekend, we each took turns sharing the details of our personal journeys. This included our childhood, pivotal moments, challenges and woundings, and especially how we sensed God weaving Himself through the fabric of our stories. That weekend, I quickly understood why I felt so drawn to the woman at my very first meeting in January. Our stories shared many poignant details, and those three days served as a springboard for a deep friendship I would soon cherish. This special retreat was a gift that each of us ladies treasured, and it served to strengthen our relationships and tender care for one another as we moved back to our normal Identity Group meetings. The Lord provided exactly what I needed in these beautiful women, before I fully understood what He would soon ask of me.

Both of us were experiencing a vital piece of the puzzle necessary as we walked further into our story - Community. A band of men to cover one another in times of fierce battle. A tribe of women to encourage and support each other through the challenges of life. Every one of us needs community. The two of us had yet to discover how this would play out in our lives, but God was knitting us into relationships that would soon become lifelines.

At some point in your story, you've most certainly encountered difficulties that feel too heavy to hold alone. Galatians 6:2 says, "Bear one another's burdens, and so fulfill the law of Christ." Having trusted people around you to help shoulder the weighty load makes burdens easier to bear. As the Body of Christ, we need one another. In the dedication of this book, we referenced a quote by Harville Hendrix directly pointing to the power of community: "We are born in relationship, we are wounded in relationship, and *we can be healed in relationship.*" You were created in the image of the triune God, a beautiful picture of relationship in action: Father, Son and comforting Spirit. You were fashioned for connection, relationship, and community. Are you embracing this valuable gift?

Your Turn:

1. There is a wonderful truth found in Ephesians 5:26 demonstrating how we can be cleansed by the washing of water with the Word. How do you engage with the Scriptures personally? What about as a couple? We encourage you to get creative here and authentically interact with God's Word, not simply to check it off your list of Christian duties. The truth of the Scriptures can cleanse and wash our mind!

2. We were created for relationships in the context of community. As a husband, are you connected to a group of men where you express yourself genuinely? As a wife, are you knit in with a group of women where you can be real? What about together - do you have other couples you can authentically share life with, back and forth? If not, how can you begin to pursue these important relationships?

3. Have either of you experienced someone helping to bear your burdens like it talks about in Galatians 6:2? Discuss what that felt like. Have you been on the other side of that equation, sharing the load of someone else's burden? How did it make you feel in that position?

CHAPTER EIGHT:
HIS WAYS ARE HIGHER

"Our God is in the heavens, and He does as He pleases." Psalm 115:3

    In the first few months of 2024, I (Clinton) engaged in weekly therapy with my CSAT, Kyle. I slowly began to soften towards the Lord, and Kyle helped me learn how to acknowledge, feel, and process my emotions for the first time in my life. It was liberating; however, I remained slightly guarded because I still had a secret to maintain. Here I was, opening up to Kyle as well as the men in my Pure Desire group, but I had to keep a careful balance. How much could I share without revealing my darkness? How could I offer transparency while protecting this thing I vowed to keep hidden? For many years, I didn't even think about that part of my story, because it wasn't ever at risk for exposure. Now, my interactions with other men, and especially Kyle, created an intention for greater caution regarding my past infidelity.

    As my therapy sessions progressed, Kyle encouraged me to consider what led me to choose sexually addictive behaviors as a way of coping throughout my life. We began to look back at life circumstances and dynamics of my family for clues. This was a bit of a relief, because the focus shifted from being centered solely on me. In April, Kyle assigned some homework. He asked me to ponder what I learned about life from a relational standpoint growing up. Of those items, what could I choose to cherish and hold onto, and what was I ready to release at this point in my life? I returned home from that session, shared my new homework with Nikki, and asked if she was willing to help me process through that sometime soon. She agreed, and we scheduled the discussion on our calendar.

I (Nikki) was also meeting with Kyle on my own to work through my feelings about Clinton's sexual struggles over the years. Kyle knew about the Disclosure Letter Clinton read to me with our sex therapist 6 months prior, and now I revealed my experience surrounding that letter. It was only a few short weeks after I found porn on Clinton's iPad, and he was still somewhat closed off about my discovery. When our sex therapist mentioned a Disclosure Letter, my mind questioned whether it was too soon, but I didn't know how to communicate that. We proceeded, but I found out through more research that we didn't actually complete the process. I would need to write an Impact Letter, then Clinton would respond with an Emotional Restitution Letter. Kyle confirmed the steps in this procedure, referring to it as a "Full Therapeutic Disclosure." That day in my therapy session, I shared that I still had this unexplained nagging feeling Clinton wasn't being fully honest with me about something. I described to Kyle how I saw Clinton softening and connecting to Jesus, as well as the men in his life. I asked him if maybe it was time for us to complete a new Disclosure journey so my mind could finally be at ease. Kyle believed it was a wise decision for both of our recovery journeys and combined healing moving forward. He gave me some paperwork to look over and said he would discuss it with Clinton in their next session together. Finally, Kyle presented the option for Clinton to take a fidelity polygraph test after reading his new Disclosure Letter to me. I quickly dismissed it and answered, "No, I don't need that." In my "Betrayal and Beyond" group, I heard women talking about these tests, and truthfully, I thought it seemed excessive. I wholeheartedly believed Clinton was willing to be honest with me at this point. Kyle expressed his professional standpoint that many men in longtime Sexual Addiction create a lifestyle of hiding and lying, and they simply aren't willing to be *completely honest* unless a polygraph exam is involved. He gave me additional information to consider, but said it was ultimately my choice. He committed to check in with me for a final decision before our Disclosure was scheduled.

In my next session with Kyle, I (Clinton) heard about the "Full Therapeutic Disclosure" process and willingly agreed. Simultaneously, my mind spun with how to cautiously connect the dots I'd already laid out over time. I was opening up to Pete, different men in my Pure Desire group, Kyle, and of course now I had to consider the things I wrote to Nikki in my original Disclosure Letter the past October. How could I fill in more details and timelines surrounding my history with porn use, while dancing around a sexual affair I was still unwilling to divulge? I would need to be very careful. With Kyle that day, I displayed openness and confidence for the road ahead of us. Besides, I'd made it these many years with my secret still intact. I just had to get through this one last bump in the road, and we could finally put the questions behind us for good.

The following weekend, Nikki and I traveled to the Pittsburgh area for a memorial service celebrating the lives of my aunt and uncle lost in a tragic home explosion several weeks prior. As we drove, I discussed my latest homework from Kyle with Nikki regarding the things I wanted to both keep and release from my upbringing. Multiple blessings came to mind as I looked back over what I learned as a child. My heritage included an entire family choosing to follow Jesus, walking by faith as we believed for the Lord's provision, learning to hear His voice early in life, and witnessing and experiencing miracles of all kinds over the years. I was richly blessed!

As I shifted attention to what I was ready to let go of, the Holy Spirit began to reveal several lies woven through the fabric of my history. (In Chapter Two, I unfolded how these lies showed up in my younger days, but at 49-years-old is when I first became aware of the ways these beliefs influenced my entire life.) The three lies Holy Spirit uncovered in that moment included:

1. "Other people struggle with those issues, I don't."
2. "I can't be wrong."
3. "I have to figure this out on my own."

The weight of this new information was heavy. I played back many scenarios throughout my existence with this new filter, and it felt overwhelming. It began to make sense why I acted the way I did, not that I was an evil or malicious guy, but these lies seemed like actual truth to me. They steered the way I lived my life, and it was a weighty realization. Nikki offered encouragement to me and gratitude to God for uncovering these destructive lies. While I was driving, she made notes on my phone during our conversation, so I could share them with Kyle at my next appointment.

The heaviness of the emotional work I was doing got compounded by the fact that we were driving right through the geography of my tumultuous teen years. That weekend, I showed Nikki the various places I lived, and I sensed the general oppression there. Add to the mix, I spent days interacting with my family of origin and much of our extended family. It was so good to be with everyone, *and* I sensed the pull towards operating from my familiar role in the family. Nikki and I purposefully stayed connected that weekend. We recognized many intense aspects at play, including the revelation of deep-rooted lies, proximity of traumatic adolescent memories, ingrained family dynamics, and we carefully walked through all of them together.

We returned from the memorial weekend in Pittsburgh, and I (Nikki) was extremely grateful to God for opening Clinton's eyes to see the three destructive lies that affected his history. The revelation was profound, and I witnessed the tenderizing result in my husband. On the long drives to and from Pennsylvania, Clinton shared deeper feelings and thoughts with me than ever before in our relationship. It solidified in my heart that it was definitely the right time to walk through the Therapeutic Disclosure together. As I considered the journey ahead, my mind drifted back to the polygraph test. I still had a negative connotation about it, and I learned through years of therapy to get curious about my strong reactions to these things. So, I grabbed my journal and opened my heart to Jesus.

These were the words I wrote to Him on Monday, April 22, 2024: "Lord, please help Clinton to be honest, open, and transparent with me and not hold back because he's trying to protect me. I need closure on that chapter of our marriage long ago. I think I need to ask for the polygraph test so I won't question Clinton, or my gut, on these things anymore. Lord, is that ok for me to request?" I took a deep breath and quieted my mind. Immediately, God responded, "Yes, my Love, ask for the polygraph. Truth will be freedom, for BOTH of you. I want you to *Trust My Process.*" I finished writing His words and closed my journal.

Now, I just had to figure out how to ask... I wrestled with it for several days. Clinton and I had a therapy session scheduled with Kyle on Thursday that week, so I decided to wait until then. If things got "sticky," I would have a mediator to help me through it.

April 25th, we met in Kyle's office to discuss final details about our new Disclosure scheduled for May 13th. Our session continued, and I felt myself growing more anxious. My resolve to ask Clinton to take a polygraph test was waning, but the Lord had my back. Kyle looked at me and inquired if I had made a final decision about asking Clinton to submit to a polygraph exam. I swallowed, and though Clinton sat to my left on the couch, I fixed my eyes straight ahead on Kyle with my answer. I explained I was initially against it, but when I took it before the Lord, He said yes, because the truth would set us both free. With a quick side glance at Clinton, I noticed his face looked white. Kyle asked Clinton what he was feeling, and he replied first that he was surprised I had time to talk to the Lord about it, but didn't mention it to him. He also said he felt anxious because he'd heard horror stories of other men's experiences with polygraph testing. Kyle gave Clinton a little more information to help set his fears at ease. Then, still looking at Kyle, I explained I thought about talking to Clinton regarding the polygraph on the ride to our appointment, but I was afraid he would be angry and think of me negatively. Kyle smiled at me and suggested I ask Clinton about that directly. I took a deep breath, turned on the couch and looked at my husband with tears brimming. "Are you upset with me for requesting a polygraph test?" He took a long deep breath, and his whole body relaxed. "No, I'm not upset with you. If the Lord said yes, then we need to do it."

We concluded our session, and Kyle gave me the polygraph examiner's contact info. He cautioned that since we were only two and a half weeks from Disclosure, this gentleman may not have an opening, but he might have an alternate contact for me. After Clinton and I returned home, I dialed his number. The examiner answered and relayed he was available immediately after our Disclosure on May 13th. My heart settled. I knew it was the Lord's way of confirming His perfect plan for us.

When the "poly-bomb" dropped in that therapy session, I (Clinton) realized this shocking new development was God's loving way of "forcing my hand." While repairing with Nikki from what she understood as the Emotional Affair, I made a silent vow to carry the truth of my many sexual sins to the grave... Unless He forced me to reveal it... Funny, I somehow thought God wouldn't hold up His end of my fragile bargain. The very moment I realized a polygraph test was imminent, something changed inside. For all those years of holding this dark secret, deep down I truly wanted an opportunity to unburden myself. Though I didn't understand it at the time, my wife requesting I submit to the polygraph was actually God's grace-filled *Invitation* to freedom for me. Finally, I was ready to answer YES to His call. I decided right then that I would humble myself and tell Nikki *the whole truth*.

I had already begun writing my new Disclosure Letter, but now I knew I had to rethink my approach. No stone unturned, nothing left in the dark. I was ready to be Radically Honest for the first time in my entire life. Nikki would be devastated, but the mere thought of walking in the Light propelled me forward. I began to understand that I couldn't walk in authentic healing and freedom in this part of my life until I allowed myself to be truly known in this part of my life. Did I really believe God was in the middle of all this? Yes, and I trusted He would give me strength.

A week later, Kyle and I met alone to discuss the progress of my letter. He greeted me with his usual "glad to be with you" smile as I took a deep breath and looked him in the eye. "Kyle, I need to ask you to forgive me, because I've lied to you. All this time, I've been hiding things that happened earlier in my marriage. The truth is, when Nikki first discovered my Emotional Affair, I made a vow to never uncover that it was also sexual in nature. I was prepared to take this to my grave. Last week, when Nikki requested that I submit to a polygraph test, I knew God was asking me to reveal everything." I sensed Kyle felt the weight of my fresh confession; however, this wasn't his first rodeo. He listened kindly as I spoke the words detailing my infidelity out loud, for the first time ever. I was 49 years old, and Kyle's ears were the very first to hear the full truth of my vulnerable story. With the new information, Kyle helped me prepare for my approaching Disclosure Letter. We talked through the appropriate balance of enough factual truth for Nikki while protecting her from more wounding than necessary in the process. As we concluded, though I felt anxiety about the path ahead of me, I experienced a measure of comfort in not hiding any longer.

After my appointment, I immediately went to have lunch with Pete. The hostess tried to seat us in the middle of the restaurant, but I knew I needed some privacy. I quickly pointed to the far end of the room, and asked if we could sit there. She obliged while the two of us made our way to a secluded table overlooking the lake. Pete was his usual jovial self, but I carried the weight of my oncoming confession. I communicated something similar to what I just finished sharing with Kyle, asking Pete to forgive me for lying about my past, then I poured out the whole truth before him. God blessed me abundantly with this dear friend, a man seasoned in holding difficult stories well. Pete graciously extended forgiveness to me as he digested my painful truth. He gently inquired, "How did Nikki take the news?" to which I explained that she didn't know yet. I relayed that I literally just told my therapist, and now he was the only other person on the planet who knew the truth. Pete asked what I planned to do? I told him about our Full Therapeutic Disclosure scheduled for May 13th, and he was relieved to hear we had a plan moving forward.

I can't emphasize enough Pete's compassionate ability to hold my story. During our lunch meeting, I experienced something profound in that man's presence. As I laid out the details of my sin, it removed what felt like boulders from deep places inside of me. Then, it was as if Pete took some of those boulders, placed them in a backpack to shoulder the weight of this difficult story *with me*. It was Galatians 6:2 in action.[1] He chose to bear this burden alongside me, and I already felt lighter. Pete demonstrated care for me, and my horrific confession of past sexual sins changed *absolutely nothing* of this man's love for me. He displayed tenderness to my weakness, just like my gracious Heavenly Father.[2]

In the course of our time together that day, Pete didn't try to fix anything or offer me counsel. He was simply glad to be with me in my suffering, taking me before the Lord in prayer aloud several times as I shared my heart with him. It was raining that day, so before we both ran to our vehicles, Pete requested that we connect once more before the Disclosure to pray together as I prepared for the challenging road ahead.

The following Tuesday, I repented, asked for forgiveness and confessed the whole truth to one of the men in my Pure Desire group. The relief was tangible as I openly revealed my story for the third time. I remembered a practice my dear friend walked out in our relationship before he passed away in 2021. Lee made a point to name the sin in his life with the full gravity of what it really was. He didn't sugar-coat things and described in vivid detail the foulness of things he was guilty of. His past example helped me view my prideful sins in the present moment, as I laid them out before others and ultimately before my precious Savior.

Soon, it would be time to confess to my wife. Over the course of our marriage, I withheld things from Nikki because I didn't think she could "handle" them. She seemed emotionally fragile in my eyes. I didn't believe the full truth of my story was safe with her, because I assumed she wasn't strong enough to hold it with me. I wasn't quite certain she could hold it now. It was possible my confession could ruin everything. I risked losing my wife, my home, my relationship with my children, my connection with friends and family, and so much more. It became increasingly evident that consequences for the secrets I held over time were now close at hand.

The night before our Disclosure, I experienced increasing heaviness as I faced questions of what the next day might bring. I was emotionally exhausted from the waiting, and ready for an early bedtime. Nikki and I stood by the serve-through near our living room and casually embraced. As usual when concluding a hug, we shared a short kiss. At that moment, it dawned on me - this may be the last opportunity I have to kiss my wife. I purposefully leaned in for one more tender kiss and held her close once more. Careful to keep my emotions in check, I waited for Nikki to release first. Then, I watched her walk away to get ready for bed. The symbolism of that moment was more than I could bear, so I went to the guest bathroom to compose my emotions. Then, I joined Nikki in bed for what could have easily been my last night by her side.

Your Turn:

1. Think back on what you learned about life from your closest relationships growing up. Of those items, what will you choose to cherish and hold onto? What are you ready to release at this point in your life? Share your answers with your spouse.

2. Have you experienced a time when things were so perfectly orchestrated that it was impossible to deny the hand of God in that circumstance? Remember and reflect on those displays of God's goodness with your spouse.

3. Separately, consider if there are details of your story that don't feel safe to share with your spouse yet. Are there specific things you don't believe your spouse could handle or hold with compassion? Take those things before Jesus and ask Him for wisdom.

GLORY FROM THE ASHES

CHAPTER NINE:
GROUND ZERO – THE OTHER HALF OF THE COIN

"Whoever conceals his transgressions will not prosper, but he who confesses and forsakes them will obtain mercy." Proverbs 28:13

    The morning of May 13, 2024, I (Clinton) woke up feeling ready for the day to be over as it barely got started. Nikki and I fixed our usual Rooibos hot tea, but I had no desire for breakfast. Worship music played in the background, and we went about our morning as time dragged on; minutes felt like hours. Nikki looked hesitant; however, she explained she was "ready." She had no idea what was coming, and I wasn't able to warn her either. How could she possibly be ready for *this*? Over and over, I released it into the Lord's capable hands. It took all of my energy to stay focused on Jesus, so I didn't completely fall apart.

We finally got into the vehicle, and I began driving the 45 minute trek to Kyle's office. Nikki started our worship playlist as she sang along peacefully. I was about to shatter my wife's existence, and she sat beside me, *singing*. I prepared my heart to lay our relationship on the altar, knowing it may not survive. As I walked toward this pivotal moment, I made the difficult decision that acceptance from Jesus was more important to me than acceptance from Nikki. If the choices from my past broke us, I would live out the remainder of my days in the Light of His goodness. I understood that my honesty didn't simply come through a decision; my honesty originated in Jesus. He is the *Way*. He is the *Truth*. He is the *Life*.[1] This day, I chose to honor God with my whole self, because I recognized I was no longer my own; my beautiful Savior paid a great price for me.[2]

About three quarters of the way to Kyle's office, I noticed the song "Goodness of God" by CeCe Winans started to play.[3] I hadn't been paying much attention to the music as I drove, but I remembered Pete told me this was his favorite worship song at the time. I began singing along, and then came the phrase, "All my life You have been faithful…" A veil lifted in my mind's eye, and I became aware of God's faithful presence throughout my story. Through every moment of loneliness, He was there. In each instance of dissatisfaction, He was there. When the lies I chose to believe directed my behaviors, He was in the midst of it all. God fiercely accepted me - not my choices, but *the real me*. As the lyrics of that song poured over my heart, it wrecked me to know the Lord's faithfulness wasn't based on my actions. I wept at the thought of His goodness running after me. Whatever happened after today, my God would not abandon me. *He* was the Faithful One.

Sometime between parking the vehicle and sitting in the waiting room, I experienced a peace and confidence that made no earthly sense. It dawned on me; God gifted me the strength I needed for exactly what He was asking me to do. Kyle called us back, and there was something about seeing this man who knew my dark past, yet he shook my hand and welcomed me with joy. It felt like water on parched ground. Nikki and I settled on the couch and after a check-in and several last-minute instructions, Kyle prayed and invited the Holy Spirit into our midst.

Then, the moment arrived.

Nikki turned toward me on the sofa, and I took one last deep breath before I spoke. My voice wavered as I began. I fully understood the pain that was imminent, but my wife remained unaware. My soul trembled knowing this devastation was the only possible way to ultimate healing. I steadily made my way through the letter, but after the section describing the extent of my sexual affair, I witnessed a vacancy in Nikki's eyes. Shock was setting in. I didn't know what else to do, so I finished reading my letter. Afterwards, I experienced a strange duality between the agony brought on by my honesty and the new blissful freedom of revealing everything. We now sat on the edge of a precipice. I felt the acceptance from the Lord, and I could only pray that someday I might have acceptance once again from my wife.

Nikki stayed in the room with Kyle to process, as I walked outside to get some fresh air. Frankly, I had to focus on not hyperventilating. It was a beautiful, warm day and I tried to sit on a park bench near the office building, but quickly realized I couldn't remain still. I had to move my body while I poured my heart out before Jesus. After a bit, I was called back in to talk with Kyle by myself. He asked how I felt, and I relayed that part of me felt extremely relieved, but the other part was undone. He assured me my emotions made sense, then let me know Nikki would come back in to ask some clarifying questions. Once he and I were finished, Kyle stood to open the door for my wife, and dread hit me. I had no idea what to expect. I couldn't bear to look at Nikki. She quietly entered and sat beside me as Kyle opened the floor for her questions. It was excruciating. I just caused her painful wounds and now we would continue disturbing the raw flesh.

Understandably, I (Nikki) had a million questions racing through my mind. I took a deep breath and looked at Clinton sitting on the couch as I walked back into Kyle's office. His eyes did not meet mine. I sat beside Clinton, and Kyle had us both check in with our emotions. Then, he welcomed my questions. Before I began, I looked at Clinton and spoke quietly, "I'm sure reading that letter was very difficult for you, and

I want to thank you for trusting me with it." He nodded and quietly replied, "Thank you for listening." Earlier, Kyle had helped me hone my questions to a few of the most fruitful for our current purposes. The difficult challenge regarding our particular circumstance was that the affair happened *so many years prior*, and Clinton just couldn't recall certain things I was curious to know. I asked several clarifying questions and after hearing his answers, I felt the numbness settle over me again. I needed to be done. I looked at Kyle and he nodded, then helped us create a plan for that evening as well as the days ahead. He asked me what I needed in order to feel safe and comfortable. Did I want Clinton to move to a hotel or sleep in our guest bedroom? I closed my eyes and thought for a moment. Then, I took a breath and spoke directly to Kyle, "This man has hurt me more deeply than any other person on the planet..." I met Clinton's eyes as tears gathered in mine then continued talking, as if to Kyle. "...*and*, he is my *person*. We've practically spent our whole lives together, and I imagine a strange comfort in having him beside me in bed tonight." Kyle assured me there was no wrong answer in this circumstance, and that it made sense I felt that way. He also said if I changed my mind, that was alright too. We set some healthy boundaries for physical contact moving forward. If I initiated any physical affection, it meant I was ready and welcomed it, but Clinton needed to ask permission before touching me in any way. Kyle instructed that my safety remained the number one priority in this part of the journey.

Clinton suggested we select a location in our home designated specifically for difficult conversations moving forward. I agreed to the idea, and we settled on the "Art Room." This used to be our daughter's bedroom but now held an easy chair and a beautiful desk Clinton made for me where I enjoyed my artistic hobbies. We committed to scheduling times to communicate when we were both in the right headspace to do so. Then, afterwards we could walk out of that room, close the door, and take a break from the big emotions and processing for a bit. Kyle thought that was a healthy suggestion, then as our session wrapped up, he prayed over us once again.

Fast forward to the polygraph test. I sat alone in the lobby for a long time, waiting for the whole thing to be over. The examiner finally called me back to review Clinton's results. My brain remained in a thick fog. I waded through his explanation of the graphs relating to various questions he asked Clinton about the Disclosure Letter and details of his affair. He told me my husband passed with "No Deception Indicated," and I just wanted to go home. Clinton was already in the car, so I walked out to meet him. My brain felt like a mass of cotton balls. As I buckled my seatbelt, I relayed the results to my husband and requested we not discuss anything further until the next morning in the Art Room. He agreed, and worship music continued in the background for the 40 minute ride home.

We arrived around 6:30pm and tried to eat something. Neither of us were very hungry, but understood caring for ourselves during this difficult time was vital. We were physically and emotionally spent, but it was too late for a nap and too early to go to bed, so I recommended we watch a show to get our minds on something different. I knew I couldn't handle anything intense or emotionally triggering, so I suggested we start back at Season One of *The Chosen*.[4] It was a TV series based on Biblical truth, and I needed help focusing on Jesus at that moment. (It soon became our ritual to watch a few episodes each evening after processing pieces of the fresh trauma during the day.) After two episodes that evening, we made our way to bed. I asked if we could listen to a selection from the "One Minute Pause" app by John Eldridge,[5] and I deliberately took comfort as I laid my head on Clinton's chest during the ten-minute recording. Afterwards, I rolled over and drifted to sleep in utter exhaustion.

PART TWO

BEING MADE NEW

The second half of this book shifts to the beautiful path of healing and growth the Lord laid out for us after Disclosure. We understand this may have been a difficult story to read thus far. If you're still with us, we are grateful for your perseverance. Now, we're honored to share the redemptive chapters of our story. Here, we begin laying out the valuable tools God gifted to us along the way. We joyfully offer them to you, so you can use the tools in your own marriage. Then, pass them on to others as well.

If you haven't answered the questions at the end of each chapter in Part One, now would be a good time to pause and do that. The activities in the first half of the book are intended to help you take an honest look at your own relationship, so you can build on the things you discovered. We prayerfully wrote Part Two with each of you in mind. May God richly bless you as you draw close to one another and draw even closer to Jesus - together.

CHAPTER TEN: HEALING BEGINS

"The hurt that broke your heart and left you trembling in the dark
Feeling lost and alone
Will tell you hope's a lie but what if every tear you cry
Will seed the ground where joy will grow
Nothing is wasted, nothing is wasted
In the hands of our Redeemer
Nothing is wasted"
~ Lyrics from Jason Gray's song "Nothing is Wasted"[1]

The day of our Disclosure marked a "line in the sand," so to speak. The next morning, we woke to the full reality and truth of our shared history for the first time ever, and it was frightening and surreal. Despite many wonderful aspects of our long-time relationship, things could never be like they were before Disclosure. As we got out of bed that day, we stepped into absolute destruction, then faced the daunting task of sorting through the wreckage. At just shy of thirty years of marriage, this was now Day One of our journey into the unknown.

We scheduled our very first discussion about the Disclosure for nine o'clock that morning in the predetermined spot in our home. (Over the course of the following days, weeks, and months, we referred to these times as "Art Room Conversations.") Before our meeting, we took time separately to prepare our hearts and minds. This initial encounter could have easily set the tone for our story moving forward, so we proceeded very carefully.

Prior to going to the Art Room, I (Clinton) pondered how I wanted to approach my upcoming discussion with Nikki. I remembered a concept represented by the acronym H.O.T. that I heard on a podcast named "Savage Marriage" by Phil and Priscilla Fretwell.[2] The couple spoke of how they committed to share Honesty, Openness, and Transparency with each other every day. I thought about those three words and realized that leading up to the Disclosure and polygraph test, I initially felt like I was "forced" to be honest about my past. Soon after, I began opening up to the men in my life and experienced a lightness as weight lifted from my chest. Nothing compared to this new experience. Then, it was time to be honest, open, and transparent with Nikki. In the preparation for my Disclosure Letter, I made a decision to bear my whole heart and speak the entire truth to my wife. As I pondered the idea of being H.O.T. with her, I thought back to hearing multiple men in my recovery group equating being honest with simply reporting the required facts about a situation. The problem was this inevitably hindered their own recovery as well as the relationships with their loved ones. "Telling the facts" with the idea of preserving isolation isn't really honesty. The note Nikki posted on the fridge months before came back to my mind - "We can only be as free as we are willing to be honest." I tasted the sweetness of freedom during Disclosure, and it propelled me forward to walk in a depth of honesty I'd never known.

Transparency in the concept of H.O.T. felt a little different. Imagine a transparent material such as glass. This substance is clear and allows objects on the other side to be seen easily. Nothing is in the way to impede the view. When Nikki discovered my porn use again in September 2023, it was important that I allow her to see into me. In a practical sense, this meant she could ask to look at my devices at any time, I gave her access to all my passwords, and we downloaded an app on our phones so she could see where I was located at any time. These weren't things she obsessed over, but in moments of concern, I let her freely view what was going on in my world. I had begun walking in transparency.

Perhaps for me, the most important of the three ideas included in H.O.T. became the openness piece. As mentioned, transparency involved allowing Nikki access to my life. Honesty was something I could willingly offer, and my wife could also ask questions expecting a truthful response from me. Openness, however, encompassed a much broader portion of this equation. To be fully open with Nikki, I needed to offer thoughts, feelings, and struggles that she would never be aware of if I didn't share them. This was the crux. Was I ready to bring vulnerable things to the table that Nikki would never know otherwise? Openness was brand new to me and would require the most practice. I chose to approach my wife for our first Art Room Conversation with vulnerability as I expressed full honesty, openness, *and* transparency.

I met Nikki at nine o'clock, and we sat facing one another. She looked at me tentatively, and I asked the Lord to meet us in our conversation. Afterwards, we both took several deep breaths, then Nikki began recounting her debrief with Kyle from the day before. Her difficult emotions ebbed and flowed, and frankly, I was relieved she was willing to talk with me at all. Nikki risked sharing her profound hurt and asked more questions about my affair. I passed a rigorous polygraph test the day before, so I could have easily been tempted to get defensive, but this was my opportunity to be H.O.T. with my wife. I vulnerably expressed my openness before Nikki and allowed her to hear the things I had hidden for so long. What a strange paradox: I held both freedom and excruciating pain at the exact same time. It was a difficult first conversation, but it felt so good to walk in the Light, before both Jesus and my wife.

As I (Nikki) spoke, Clinton listened intently and made notes in his journal. I vacillated between tears, anger, confusion, and numbness. It was challenging to look my husband in the eye and ask the terrible questions banging around in my head. Because the affair was so long ago, I questioned everything about our history in the time between then and the present. What was real? Were we actually happy during all these years? How could those horrible things my husband did really be true? I came to a pause in my thoughts and realized I'd been talking for a long time. I looked at Clinton and asked what he was thinking. He took a deep breath and responded, "I will definitely share my thoughts and feelings with you, but right now, it's important that you feel *heard*." I immediately started to cry. This was so new and different for us. We had no history of sharing painful emotions, let alone sitting kindly with one another in the middle of them. My husband showed no defensiveness or justification for his past. He simply looked at me with tenderness and conveyed that he was willing to hear how his choices destroyed me. It was overwhelming as I received his loving care for me in my fragile state.

After about two hours, we came to a natural stopping point and Clinton prayed again. He asked God to seal our time and begin the process of healing our hearts. We each previously scheduled a lunch meeting for that day with someone we considered close and safe. Clinton met with Pete, while I went to connect with my dear friend from my Identity Group. Those two brought a source of great encouragement, love, support, and beautiful care to each of us in our broken state. It felt comforting to be seen, heard, and known by these friends in the midst of our devastation as we took the first step toward healing in our marriage.

In the first days after Disclosure, I faced a shattering truth: Our wedding vows had been broken long ago, and our marriage covenant was no longer intact. With a heavy heart and many tears, I removed my wedding ring. Though I had Biblical grounds for divorce due to my husband's infidelity, that was not my heart's desire. I still loved this man, deeply. I wanted to remain with him; however, it would require completely starting over. Many words came to mind in light of our situation: repair, restore, rebuild, recover… None of them seemed to fit. Our marriage was decimated down to the foundation. All we had left was Jesus. There would be no recycling of any building materials from before May 13th. *Everything* had to be NEW. At the same time, I didn't intend to throw away the past three decades as if they held no value. We were blessed with two amazing children and a host of treasured memories. Regardless, we returned to two separate individuals, beginning fresh. I intended to allow the Lord to expose all our relational dysfunction as we walked together toward health, and eventually, a brand-new marriage covenant.

For the first two weeks, we shared many tough Art Room Conversations, and multiple therapy sessions, both separately and together. Thankfully, we ran our own business and were able to take time off to focus solely on healing. We saw the Lord's hand at work as we utilized the many tools presented to us by our therapists, Kyle and Monica. It was nothing short of a miracle that we used these aids, because our history involved poor communication and unwillingness to use tools when they were needed most. God's beautiful grace poured over us abundantly during that raw season.

One valuable concept we included in our Art Room Conversations was paying attention to something called "Relational Circuits." You can find more detail on this concept in Chris Coursey's book *The Joy Switch*,[3] and the following is a brief overview for our purposes. God created each one of us in the context of relationship. The Trinity displays a beautiful picture of our God in relationship: Father, Son, and Holy Spirit. In the first chapter of Genesis, we read that God fashioned us according to His very own relational image. How wonderful that He designed us for connection! Our brains were crafted with these Relational Circuits (RC's) that turn on and off like a light switch. When our RC's are on, we are positioned to relate well with another person. Sometimes we're unaware when we go "off-line" and wonder why we feel distant from someone we normally enjoy, like our spouse. Other times, we recognize when we feel edgy and disconnected, but don't know what to do about it. The two of us created a new habit of checking our RC's before (and sometimes even during) potentially challenging conversations. We practiced a simple litmus test denoted by the acronym C.A.K.E. found in the book *The 4 Habits of Joy-filled Marriages: How 15 Minutes a Day Can Help You Stay in Love*.[4] This book taught us that if we remain Curious, Appreciative, Kind, and share Eye Contact, our RC's will most likely stay on. When we notice any of these four clues becoming more difficult, it's probably because the switch to our Relational Circuits flipped to the "off" position. If this happens, we can simply pause our interaction and care for ourselves in order to openly reconnect with one another. We will offer practical applications for the concept of RC's at the end of this chapter, so stay tuned.

Another precious resource in those challenging first weeks of our journey was a practice called "Active Listening." There are many explanations and different ways to approach this tool. We chose the one found in Clifford and Joyce Penner's book *Restoring the Pleasure* where the authors describe this concept as follows: "Active Listening includes looking and listening carefully, reading 'body language' for feelings expressed, and putting yourself in another person's shoes (empathy)."[5] The two of us practiced the Penner's format of going back and forth between one spouse as the speaker and the other as the listener. (It's important to check your RC's to confirm both of you are ready for a particular discussion. Otherwise, it's easy to talk over each other, shut down, or experience heightened emotions in the process, which defeats the purpose of Active Listening.)

We'll describe an example process here with the husband as the speaker and the wife as the listener. In the first step, the husband gathers his thoughts and feelings, then communicates them clearly and openly with his wife. The second step involves the wife laying her own reactions and responses down in order to mirror back what she understood her husband was conveying. (We find it helpful to use the phrase, "So, what I'm hearing you say is…") In the third step of the progression, the husband can either affirm her interpretation or bring more clarity to what he's trying to communicate. Once the husband feels understood in his initial subject, this three-step process begins again for the wife to respond with her thoughts and feelings on his topic. This whole progression can be repeated in as many back-and-forth cycles as necessary until a particular subject is resolved or as long as both spouses feel connected with their Relational Circuits on. (A word of wisdom here: You may not exhaust a particular topic in one sitting. If either spouse's RC's flicker or turn off, care for yourselves and pause to reconnect, or take a break until a later time.) It may seem "clunky" at first, but the more you practice Active Listening, the more it becomes natural to listen, hear, and understand one another's point of view in a loving manner.

As you can imagine, checking our RC's and practicing Active Listening became vital tools as the two of us entered a brand-new phase of our relationship after Disclosure. We experienced a multitude of challenging discussions, all fraught with big emotions that had the potential to flood one or both of us with pain and distress. These two simple resources, along with our commitment to be H.O.T. with each other every day, provided a stable and firm foundation where we could begin building our new relationship

Your Turn:

1. Breathing is an overlooked and underutilized tool to help regulate yourself when you experience emotions ranging from overwhelmed to shut down. There are a myriad of breathing techniques you can research on your own, but our favorite is simple and effective. Take a slow breath in through your nose, completely filling your lungs. Then, let your breath out even more slowly with your lips pursed as if you are blowing out a candle. Now, on your own, first assess how you feel, then close your eyes and count out 5-10 deep breaths. Do you feel calmer? At some point, try holding hands with your spouse or even embracing, then take 5-10 deep breaths together in unison. What do you notice?

2. In this chapter, we've introduced the concept of keeping your Relational Circuits (RC's) on while interacting with your spouse. If you'll remember, we referred to Chris Coursey's acronym C.A.K.E. to check if you are ready to connect with one another. Ask yourself the following questions to check your RC's before moving on: Can I approach my spouse with *Curiosity*? Am I able to *Appreciate* my spouse and their perspective? Will I treat my spouse with *Kindness*? Can I hold loving *Eye Contact* with my spouse? Once you feel relationally connected, take turns answering the following: What is one thing you are not looking forward to in the coming week, and what is one thing you anticipate with joy this week?

3. Active Listening is a three-step process you can use to help speak clearly, listen with empathy, and ultimately communicate more effectively. If you'll remember, the progression begins with the speaker openly sharing their perspective for discussion. Then, the listener mirrors back what they are hearing, and finally, the speaker confirms or further clarifies their point. After that, switch speaker and listener to continue with another cycle. Check to make sure both you and your spouse have RC's on, then utilize Active Listening to discuss something relatively simple like where you'd like to go to dinner on date night or how to determine who will help the kids with normal tasks this evening. After practicing several less complicated topics to get the hang of it, consider scheduling a time to use Active Listening to discuss Question #3 from Chapter Four: What foxes do you need to catch *now* to keep your vineyard safe?

CHAPTER ELEVEN:
STEPPING TOWARD FORGIVENESS

"In a word, live together in the forgiveness of your sins, for without it no human fellowship, least of all marriage, can survive." ~ Dietrich Bonhoeffer

In the two weeks after Disclosure, I (Nikki) prepared my Impact Letter to Clinton. As we processed together through therapy sessions and many Art Room Conversations, I took time to assess all the areas of my life touched by Clinton's Sexual Addiction. Kyle provided worksheets to help me understand how Clinton's porn use and especially the sexual affair affected me relationally, psychologically, emotionally, physically, spiritually, and much more. In my sessions, Kyle noticed a tendency for me to "soften" or sugar-coat my words and emotions regarding Clinton's past. He encouraged me that it was extremely important to express my authentic thoughts and feelings about my husband's choices in the Impact Letter. This was an opportunity to lay out the detailed offenses Clinton's sexual behaviors caused that would require his genuine apology to me, repentance before the Lord, and making amends in our relationship over time.

The Impact Letter was heart-rending to write, and even more agonizing to read to my husband. On May 27, 2024, exactly two weeks after his Disclosure Letter to me, I spoke the words of my letter aloud to Clinton. It was challenging to stay present and connected, but we both utilized tools to remain emotionally regulated while keeping our Relational Circuits (RC's) on. A few times during the letter when he noticed the numbness returning in my voice or expression, Clinton encouraged me to pause and take a few deep breaths. He reminded me this was a vital step in recovery for both of us, and we shouldn't rush through it. It was excruciating to say out loud the gut-wrenching cries of my heart; definitely the hardest thing I'd ever done.

I tapped into my true identity and used my voice to express the details of what I needed from Clinton to move forward in our relationship. I communicated healthy boundaries, things I would do and things I asked of my husband, in order to feel safe with him. As I concluded my Impact Letter, I assured Clinton that I still loved him, and I committed to eventually forgive him, but let him know I wasn't ready to do that yet. It was extremely important not to rush the process of authentic forgiveness. All those years ago, I quickly "forgave" my husband for what I believed was an Emotional Affair, out of fear and insecurity. That *would not* happen again. I needed time to understand the full truth and gravity of what I was actually forgiving, along with weighing the heavy cost of Clinton's choices.

Though very difficult to hear, I (Clinton) knew I needed Nikki's honest, open, and transparent words describing the painful repercussions my actions created over time. Something I heard in my Pure Desire group helped me as I prepared for my wife's Impact Letter. I was made aware that it was vital for me to hear the blunt facts of what my betrayals caused, so I could begin to experience genuine empathy for Nikki. If she withheld her deepest thoughts and feelings, I could never be fully in touch with the heartbreaking gravity of our situation. I learned that in any type of addiction, empathy skills are naturally stunted. Looking back over our marriage, I had to admit I consistently avoided putting myself in Nikki's shoes, and I ignored potential ramifications so I could continue my addictive patterns. So, her Impact Letter was exactly that - my wife putting voice to the *shattering impact* of my Sexual Addiction on her mind, body, spirit, and so much more. It was imperative that I heard her heart.

Understanding the importance of this step in our healing journey, I paid close attention to my own emotional state, as well as Nikki's, as she read her letter. I knew this level of brutal honesty and raw emotion was foreign for both of us, so I carefully watched for signs of disconnection. In moments when I noticed my wife's hesitation or I heard the numbness in her voice, I gently encouraged her to pause and take a few breaths. I assured Nikki I wasn't going anywhere and she could take all the time she needed. As she regulated and calmed, I did the same. It wasn't easy to hear the traumatic consequences I inflicted on the woman before me, but so necessary for my recovery as well as hers.

When Nikki finished reading her Impact Letter, I thanked her for sharing it with me. I looked at her as tears welled in my eyes and conveyed that I *heard* her. She said how difficult it was to say all those things out loud, and it would have been easier to hold them inside. I assured my wife I needed to hear every word, and as tears fell down my cheeks, I told her, "This is going to help me be a better man."

Upon hearing those words, I (Nikki) began to cry again too. I told Clinton I couldn't believe all this was true and I *didn't want* to believe it was true either. After a few moments, I looked at him and asked him to tell me "The thing." Several days prior, Clinton said the phrase, "We're gonna make it" and in difficult moments, I requested his reassurance once again. This was one of those moments. My husband sat facing me and cried as he communicated, "We're gonna make it. I'm gonna make it. You're gonna make it... With God's help, *we will make it through this*." I reached for Clinton's hand and invited him to stand as I melted into his embrace. The floodgates opened and the two of us clung to one another as we wept mournfully.

Eventually we quieted, and I stayed in my husband's arms while we breathed in unison, deeply and slowly. Then, I looked up at him with a sad smile and inquired what he needed after hearing my letter. He responded that he wanted to take a walk, to move his body. I asked if he preferred to be alone, but Clinton believed it would feel better to be *with* me. We got our shoes on, and I took my husband's hand as we quietly walked our wooded driveway together.

I (Clinton) received a copy of Nikki's Impact Letter, and over the course of the next three days, I spent chunks of time alone in the Art Room writing my reply called an Emotional Restitution Letter. This would be a direct response to Nikki's thoughts and emotions on how my choices and behaviors impacted her. I prayerfully considered each individual offense she listed in her letter, as well as the description of how it made her feel. As I wrote, I brought each sin before the Lord, humbled myself, and repented at His feet. Before I could ever hope to experience forgiveness from my wife, I needed to walk in the forgiveness of my Savior. My time with Jesus was painful yet precious, and I encountered His redemptive work in me while I wrote this second important letter to Nikki. Those three days were emotionally intense as I prepared to express my genuine apology and repentance to this woman I truly loved.

May 30th was the day scheduled for Clinton's Emotional Restitution Letter, and at dawn, I (Nikki) woke up to unprompted intrusive thoughts about his affair. This had become a regular occurrence and made mornings the most difficult part of my day. Upon rousing, I voiced the disturbing images to Clinton that bombarded me yet again, and he gently suggested we try a new morning routine. We stepped out of bed and as I got dressed for the day, my husband found our foldable camp chairs and set them up in our nearly empty formal living room. When I came out of the bedroom, I noticed my chair was facing one direction. The arm of his camp chair touched the arm of my chair, but it sat facing the complete opposite direction. Clinton stood holding two mugs of our favorite hot tea and welcomed me to our new "Conversation Chairs."

We sat face to face in our strangely situated camp chairs, sipping our tea as we experienced something extremely unusual. So soon after exposing his sexual sins, Clinton could have easily avoided my gaze in guilt and shame, but he purposefully humbled himself and connected to me through eye contact. Likewise, in my freshly wounded state, refraining from looking at my husband's eyes made sense, but I also chose humility and fixed my eyes on his. Clinton and I encountered the abundant grace of the Lord in those moments. We now understand that we stumbled upon something exceptional in those simple camp chairs in the middle of our living room that morning.

Clinton explained the Conversation Chairs also allowed us to face each other so we could share joy like Monica taught me the week before in my therapy session. The concept of Sharing Joy is one of the 19 Relational Skills detailed in Chris Coursey's book *Transforming Fellowship*.[1] The general idea is that as we look someone in the eye and genuinely convey that we're happy to be in their presence, joy has the opportunity to grow between us. Furthermore, the book *The Other Half of Church* talks about how "God designed our brains to run on joy like a car runs on fuel."[2] Clinton and I found ourselves in a season requiring all the joy we could collect! As we practiced sharing joy in our Conversation Chairs each morning, the capacity to handle our challenging circumstances expanded, and my intrusive thoughts of the affair lessened over time. (A few months later, we bought two comfortable recliners to replace our camp chairs in the living room. These side-by-side recliners facing in opposite directions always provide a curious source of discussion when new folks visit our home! At the time of this writing, Clinton and I still enjoy moments of connection in our Conversation Chairs every day –see photo.)

Later that day, I (Clinton) planned to share my Emotional Restitution Letter with Nikki - the final step in our Full Therapeutic Disclosure process. My emotions felt raw and slightly untethered. Over the days of preparation, had I really processed true repentance with Jesus? Did I understand that His forgiveness was enough, even if my wife couldn't move past my betrayals against her? I held the tension between nerves over Nikki's response to my letter and trusting God's ultimate plan for the two of us.

As with her Impact Letter three days before, Nikki and I approached our time together with prayer, checking our RC's, and pausing as needed to remain present and connected. Full of emotion, I slowly read the letter to my wife while purposefully looking in her eyes.

Each individual section acknowledged the excruciating pain Nikki endured at my hand, and I conveyed my genuine apology, repentance, and hope for her eventual forgiveness. For each offense, I vulnerably opened myself and shared deep sorrow for the devastation I caused in our marriage. I conveyed to my wife that I understood my actions destroyed our relationship, and as a result, we both faced the burden of completely starting over. Using the vows from our wedding day, I humbly admitted how I broke those promises that I made to her almost thirty years prior. With sincerity, I expressed my full commitment to walking with Nikki and Jesus toward a NEW covenant with NEW vows, in His perfect timing.

When I finished, Nikki took hold of my hands and with tears she thanked me for my words. Then, she prayed for God's grace as we stepped into the next phase of our healing journey together. We stood, thanked the Lord for His perfect plan, and held each other close as we wept once again. This time, with hope.

Your Turn:

1. Our Conversation Chairs were a creative way to come together in a manner that was physically different than before, and it literally forced us to shift our perspective. Is there a recurring topic of conversation in your marriage that would benefit from a fresh approach? Like our Art Room Conversations, would it be beneficial for you to reserve a specific location to have important discussions? Where could that be? Maybe even set up some Conversation Chairs of your own!

2. The two of us learned and practiced the vital skill of Sharing Joy regularly throughout our healing journey. The books we mention in this chapter go into much more detail, but here's the overall concept: Sit facing one another closely and hold eye contact while you express non-verbal *gladness to be together* with your spouse. Do this for a few seconds, then close your eyes to take a short break. After a moment (and maybe a deep breath), return to joy-filled eye to eye connection once again. We like to do 5-6 cycles at a sitting. It may feel awkward at first. That's ok, keep practicing! You may even laugh sometimes. Authentic joy is contagious, and it feels so good to share it with one another!

3. In our human nature, it's natural to portray ourselves in the best light possible. With the positives in our life, we tend to display them readily. Regarding sinful aspects, we often minimize or hide to look better in front of others. Is there an area of your life that you've been "sugar-coating" that you need to face and actually name as *sin*?

CHAPTER TWELVE: MOVING AT WARP SPEED

"Then shall your light break forth like the dawn, and your healing shall spring up speedily..." Isaiah 58:8a

      As we begin this chapter, the two of us want to remind you of the words from our Preface that this is NOT a book detailing how to repair after infidelity or Sexual Addiction. We are telling *our story*. God invited the two of us into an intense and fast-paced journey of restoration. Several times in the beginning of our recovery, the Lord spoke that He was doing an expedited work in us. Our season of life and work situation provided the time and space to spend extended periods everyday with Jesus and each other as we healed very rapidly. Don't confuse our unusual timeline with your ability to utilize the principles we share. We listened for the voice of Jesus every day as He unfolded *His perfect path for us*. We encourage you to do the same. Every marriage journey will look differently, and we are simply using our personal story to share the tools and concepts we learned on the way to Spiritual

Intimacy with one another and with Jesus. No matter the pace, it's vital that you *make time* to connect. Growth doesn't happen all on its own. You must create margin in your lives and be proactive if you truly desire change.

In early June 2024, I (Clinton) heard the Lord reveal a step-by-step plan for me and Nikki, including grieving, wooing, courting, engagement, and finally, a new marriage covenant. First in the process, we faced a time of grieving. This entailed separately working through hurt from the past and counting the cost of our painful history. We each needed to feel the gravity of what we were walking through. This season also encompassed grieving together and not holding this heavy load of sorrow alone. It was vital for my recovery to see and hear Nikki's grief and she also needed to experience mine. Over time, we came to understand that grieving is not a linear process, and it often comes in waves at unexpected moments. This type of sorrow usually flows more like a spiral, and we repeatedly circled back around to work through more of the complex feelings stirred through various life circumstances. After the Disclosure, Nikki's Impact Letter, and my Emotional Restitution Letter, we entered this weighty season of grief that ebbed and flowed for quite some time as we moved forward together.

Next in the plan, the Lord spoke to me regarding "wooing" Nikki once again. My sexual indiscretions, along with hiding and lying about them for years, shattered our relationship as well as my wife's trust in me. The nature of any addictive behavior is selfishness and isolation, so I needed to start back at the beginning, preferring and caring for Nikki. Simple things like opening her car door, bringing her a cold drink, or helping to put her jacket on consistently remained in the forefront of my mind. I smiled at her tenderly and connected regularly in conversation. Also, to build trust again, I continued to focus on being H.O.T. (Honest, Open, and Transparent) with my wife. I allowed her access to my mind and heart, *especially* regarding repairing my relationship with Jesus. After Nikki started feeling safe with me again and trust slowly returned, the Lord said we could begin a season of courting (before moving on to engagement and eventually a new marriage covenant).

The first week of June, I (Nikki) continued several practices for daily connection with Jesus that proved to be a lifeline throughout my healing journey. One of the devices I used was the "One Minute Pause" app with John Eldridge at *Wild at Heart* Ministries.[1] Clinton and I discovered this app when I was in the middle of my personal therapy adventure in 2022. The various meditations available in this tool include soothing music, stunning nature visuals, helpful breathing techniques, and beautiful Scriptural truth. The "Pauses" helped me release my burdens to the Lord according to 1 Peter 5:7 which says, "Cast all your anxiety on Him because He cares for you." After the Disclosure experience, my world was fraught with the potential for anxious thoughts, and I had to intentionally keep my focus on the Lord just to get through the day. Many times, I found a quiet spot and listened to the meditations, imagining Jesus right there with me. After Disclosure, Clinton and I regularly laid in bed at night and played a Pause to help settle our minds before drifting off to sleep. Both of us utilized these beneficial Pauses during our recovery. It was crucial that we kept our minds and hearts positioned toward Jesus as we healed, and the "One Minute Pause" app was a valuable tool to keep us centered on Him.

Another life changing practice I used to stay close to the Lord was a type of journaling Monica introduced me to from a book titled *Joyful Journey; Listening to Immanuel.*[2] She shared about these techniques when I first met her in January 2024. I immediately bought and read the book, then started enjoying what the authors refer to as "Immanuel Journaling" regularly. I began with something they call "Interactive Gratitude." The authors provide a simple explanation in chapter three of their book: "There are two parts in interactive gratitude. First, we give thanks to God; second, we slow down to perceive how God responds to our gratitude."[3] So, I would grab my journal and favorite pen and pour out my thanksgiving and praise to the Lord on the paper. After a few sentences (or even a couple of paragraphs), I stopped to wait before Him and listen for His still, small voice. Then, I wrote down His words of love back to me. It helped to imagine how a parent might speak to a young child who just expressed their own excitement and joy. As long as the perception of God's words lined up with Scripture and didn't contradict His character, I received them with peace. From January to June, I regularly took time to express my heart to Jesus and receive His words of love back to me. It was a delightful and fulfilling spiritual discipline! I shared what I was doing with Clinton along the way and encouraged him to try it sometime. Journaling of any sort was challenging for him due to a lifelong battle with dyslexia, so he seemed reluctant.

Several times before Disclosure, I asked if I could read my Immanuel Journaling to Clinton, and he was open to it. As I shared from my journal, first my expressions to the Lord and then His precious responses, it opened a whole new experience of how the words on the page ministered to me. I found it incredibly vulnerable to speak God's heart toward me out loud, for my husband to hear. I hoped he might join me someday, but I understood he wasn't ready yet. I chose to leave it in God's hands.

Clinton shared the step-by-step path the Lord revealed for the two of us, and I recognized his purposeful means of "wooing" me. He was gentle and kind, intentionally offering acts of service that I enjoyed. He also connected emotionally with me and started meaningful conversations to foster closeness between us. My husband respected my boundaries with physical affection, and either waited for my initiation or asked permission to touch me in any way. Clinton's tender pursuit felt good to me. Soon, I realized I *wanted* his arm around me as we watched *The Chosen* episodes each evening. When he looked into my eyes with care for my feelings, I *desired* his loving embrace. Our friendship was blossoming; however, I still needed to see and hear his authentic repair with Jesus in order to fully trust and feel safe with him again.

On June 6, 2024, I stepped out in faith and asked Clinton if he was willing to do some Immanuel Journaling with me. He was hesitant, but said he would give it a try. We settled in our Conversation Chairs and played some instrumental music in the background. (William Augusto is an artist who provided the music for the "One Minute Pause" app,[4] and his various instrumental worship albums became the soundtrack for many aspects of healing in our marriage.) We finished the exercise, and I inquired if Clinton was open to reading his journal entry to me. He answered that he would someday soon, but he wasn't quite ready for that step. I respected his response and patiently waited while he continued walking out his personal recovery.

About a week later, I gently suggested we do more Immanuel Journaling together. Clinton agreed and before we played the worship music and got started, he offered to read his previous entry to me. It blessed me abundantly to hear his openness before the Lord, as well as his raw vulnerability to share the words he heard from Jesus with me. Knowing Clinton's utter frustration with writing due to dyslexia, his willingness to partake in this practice spoke volumes of his commitment to our healing together. The following was Clinton's very first Immanuel Journal entry:

"Lord, I'm grateful for Nikki and I being able to laugh and still be funny at times. I appreciate the tools that we've been given to help with our relationship..."

"Clinton, oh the stories we will tell together! The abandonment of yourself and the filling of Me will make the greatest of tales! It's time to pour out and be broken before others, that they may see Me and not your impersonation of Me. I want your brokenness. I love you, and I want time with you..."

I thanked my husband for speaking those words aloud and told him it meant so much to me. He smiled softly, then we took the time to each write a new interaction with Jesus in our journals. Afterwards, we openly shared them with one another, and it filled my heart with indescribable joy!

I (Clinton) want to break into the story for a moment to convey what a miracle my choice to journal actually was. Putting pen to paper has always been excruciating for me. Letters get jumbled in my mind and on the page. Even simple words start correctly in my brain, but confusion sets in when they flow from my pen. The idea of Immanuel Journaling seemed like a recipe for disaster to me. I felt convinced this was an exercise I could do a few times to demonstrate my commitment to Nikki in our recovery, but I never thought it would go beyond that. Let me be clear, the first few times of journaling didn't result in my "singing its praises." Sure, I saw the benefit but never imagined it would become a long-term practice. I noticed the miraculous shift when Nikki and I were multiple entries in, and I experienced actual anticipation building for our next journalling encounter! You might say I grew to love this spiritual discipline, but I hesitate to even call it that. Jesus extended an invitation to me through Immanuel Journaling, and as I answered YES, I found my joy being made complete in the midst of it. As I participated *with Jesus*, these fulfilling times no longer felt like a discipline in any way. Despite my difficult struggles with dyslexia, I filled page after page in my journal with conversations between me and Jesus. Just as I was wooing Nikki, He was wooing me.

I (Nikki) noticed the change in Clinton. He was opening up to the Lord more and more. It seemed as if he genuinely enjoyed Immanuel Journaling after several sessions. Journaling together in our Conversation

Chairs and openly reading the words aloud became very precious to me. It gave me hope for our future. Clinton's Sexual Addiction took a toll on his relationship with Jesus, so hearing the authentic emotion in his voice as he read to me brought comfort to my heart. I no longer walked alone in my relationship with the Lord; Clinton was right there by my side.

In mid-June, I began feeling closer to Clinton. We definitely had a long way to go in our healing process, but I felt ready for the next step. One afternoon, I approached my husband with a smile and a slight shrug of the shoulder as I offered, "Maybe you should ask me on a date..." He smiled back at me and inquired if I was available that evening. I laughed and answered yes, so Clinton planned a special outing for the two of us. We got dressed up and enjoyed our very first date together in our *new* relationship. Over the course of the next two weeks, we had several more intentional date nights, and things slowly began to feel right again.

Your Turn:

1. The "One Minute Pause" app was a beneficial tool to help redirect our minds back to Jesus. We utilized it often, both separately and together. Consider downloading this free app and find a quiet spot to listen to a Pause together. (You may also enjoy the "30 Days to Resilient" program on the same app, which includes a month of morning and evening meditations.)

2. Each of you grab some paper or journal and a pen, sit in a quiet spot free of distractions, and try your hand at Interactive Gratitude. Take a few moments separately to express your thanksgiving to God in written form. It doesn't have to be extravagant or extensive. Write specific things you want to thank the Lord for that are fresh on your mind. Then, imagine how He might respond to your gratitude and write those things below your entry. Keep it personal. What do you think Jesus would say to you? What endearing names might He call you? How would He express His love for you in this moment?

3. Then, the best part: After you finish, read your original expression of gratitude, along with the response from Jesus, *out loud* to your spouse. This is vulnerability in action! When you're done, describe how the experience made you feel - good, bad, or indifferent is perfectly fine. The goal is to practice authenticity with one another. (Pro tip: Don't stop short by only trying one Immanuel Journaling encounter! Each new entry presents an opportunity for deeper intimacy with Jesus and your spouse. More on this to come!)

CHAPTER THIRTEEN: A NEW COVENANT

"'Therefore, a man shall leave his father and mother and hold fast to his wife, and the two shall become one flesh.' This mystery is profound, and I am saying that it refers to Christ and the church. However, let each one of you love his wife as himself, and let the wife see that she respects her husband." Ephesians 5:31-33

As we progressed through our healing journey, I (Clinton) heard the Lord continue speaking to me concerning how to effectively lead and be the head of our home. This concept was nerve-racking to me, because after Disclosure, I wondered if Nikki was even open to the idea of submitting to my lead. Our history regarding spiritual authority in the home was riddled with dysfunction. Throughout our marriage, my wife talked about her desire for me to lead our family. The problem was I didn't actually know how to do that properly, but due to the lies I believed all my life, I wasn't going to ask anyone for help or guidance either. That would mean I struggled with something, and I avoided being found lacking at all costs. So, I tried to lead my family with very few skills and even less humility to reach out for assistance. Inevitably, Nikki experienced discomfort or impatience with my lack of authentic leadership, and she stepped in to take over. I perceived this as disrespectful and controlling. We both avoided conflict of any kind, so I quietly smoldered in resentment while my wife wore the "spiritual pants" in our family.

I had very little understanding of what it meant to be the Godly head in my marriage, or how it looked to cover my wife spiritually. The Lord began opening my eyes to His perfect design for leadership, found in His Word. I read in 1 Corinthians 11:3, "I want you to understand that the head of every man is Christ, the head of a wife is her husband, and the head of Christ is God." It became clear to me that all those years I tried to exert leadership over Nikki while missing the vital step of submitting my *entire life* to Jesus first. Without being covered by Christ, I could never genuinely cover my wife. So, we walked in a disordered relationship, with me feeling frustrated and Nikki feeling unsafe.

As I pressed in to hear more from the Lord, He rapidly started downloading truth to me regarding Biblical leadership. God unfolded four different spheres where I, as a husband, needed to cover my wife. They included areas I could offer protection to Nikki, comfort her, be a support to her and apply my covering to her life. Within these four categories of leadership, God showed me they each contained physical, relational, and spiritual expressions. Excited about what God was imparting, I retrieved paper and pencil. I drew 4 large circles on a blank sheet of paper, and labeled them Protection, Comfort, Support, and Application. I divided each circle into 3 equal pie pieces, then gave the individual segments a heading of Physical, Relational, and Spiritual. At this point, the Lord brought multiple examples to mind that fit into the categories of the twelve different segments until I filled all four circles on the paper (see Figure).

I immediately felt overwhelmed. How could I possibly do all the things God was asking of me? Was I really able to cover my wife after thirty years of lack in this area? How could I please God, please Nikki, and do all this right? I felt weary before I even began, and despair landed hard.

COVERING

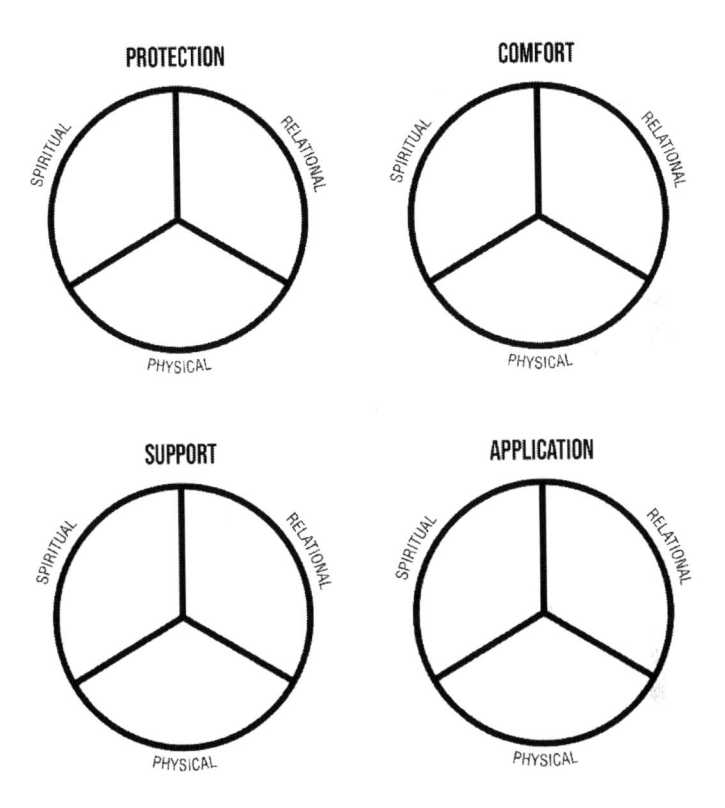

PROTECTION
SPIRITUAL / RELATIONAL / PHYSICAL

COMFORT
SPIRITUAL / RELATIONAL / PHYSICAL

SUPPORT
SPIRITUAL / RELATIONAL / PHYSICAL

APPLICATION
SPIRITUAL / RELATIONAL / PHYSICAL

That evening, I showed the paper to Nikki regarding what God revealed to me about Biblical covering. She seemed intrigued and excited to talk it over with me. She offered several more practical examples for each circle that would speak to her personally. As insightful as Nikki's suggestions were, they only caused more trepidation in my heart as I considered my mounting responsibilities in this area. I vulnerably voiced my concerns regarding how to actually walk this out, and Nikki suggested some Immanuel Journaling so I could share my thoughts with Jesus. She started William Augusto's instrumental worship music, and as I put pen to paper, a phrase appeared that changed my perspective entirely. *"Do with, not for."*

Immediately, I remembered the words from Galatians 5:25, "If we live by the Spirit, let us also keep in step with the Spirit." It connected in my mind that if I am walking ahead of or falling behind what the Spirit is doing, I am not actually *with* Him. On the other hand, being nestled in beside Him and participating in what He is doing places me in a posture of being *with* the Spirit of God. This is even further demonstrated in Matthew 11:28-30. "Come to Me, all who labor and are heavy laden, and I will give you rest. Take My yoke upon you, and learn from Me, for I am gentle and lowly in heart, and you will find rest for your souls. For My yoke is easy and My burden is light." I realized I'd spent my entire life trying to prove myself in three ways: 1) I was doing things *for* Jesus to receive His approval, 2) I was doing things *for* Jesus to receive others' approval, and 3) I was doing things *for* Jesus for my own benefit, to feel good about myself. Talk about a heavy burden! When Jesus invited me to do *with* Him and not *for* Him, I began to understand how my burden could truly become light.

In that same journal entry with the *"Do with, not for"* revelation, God spoke to me about the next step forward in my relationship with Nikki. He required me to actively cover her based on what He revealed to me about spiritual headship before I could ask her to marry me again. I questioned how I would determine when that was, and the Lord graciously responded that Nikki would let me know. So, I stepped out in faith hoping she would one day recognize her safety in my new genuine submission to Jesus.

June 25, 2024 marked our 30th wedding anniversary. Under normal circumstances, this momentous occasion might be celebrated with a grand party or an elaborate vacation. We, however, were commemorating our decision to stay married. As the day approached, I (Nikki) believed there was merit in celebrating how far we'd come in our healing. I also had increasing hope for our future together, so I suggested we plan to go out for a nice dinner. When the day finally arrived, I chose a dress from my closet and took the time to do my nails. After curling my hair and applying makeup, I put my heels on and went to the great room to sit on the couch. We still had about thirty minutes before we needed to leave, so Clinton sat in the easy chair across the room, and we chatted casually for a bit.

As we conversed, I caught a glimpse of Clinton's Covering paper on the end table beside me. I picked it up and looked carefully at each circle. Four different areas for a husband to cover his wife, each broken into thirds for physical, relational, and spiritual examples. I skimmed the words on the page when suddenly, it hit me: Clinton had been displaying many of the ideas on that paper. I voiced my revelation to him and read aloud at least a dozen ways I had experienced his Biblical leadership over me recently. You see, covering was a missing ingredient in our relationship up to this point. Clinton hadn't lived his life completely submitted under the covering of the Lord; therefore, he couldn't offer the authentic spiritual covering I truly desired. Now, after relaying phrase after phrase to Clinton regarding his new expressions of leadership, I explained how absolutely safe this made me feel.

Upon speaking of my safety, Clinton stood up and silently walked toward our bedroom. It seemed odd, but I patiently waited for him to return. After a moment, he came back into the great room and positioned himself directly in front of me. Then, he slowly got down on one knee. Clinton tenderly held out the wedding ring I'd removed after Disclosure. My heart beat rapidly as I looked at his face. Tears welled in his eyes as he began to speak, his voice thick with emotion. "Nichole Renee Mitchell, will you marry me?" He put his other hand on his chest and continued, "I mean *me*. Will you marry this NEW guy?..." Clinton's proposal included his desire to create a brand-new life together, along with his commitment to keep Jesus at the center of our relationship. Tears were plentiful for both of us as I happily whispered, "Yes." He placed the ring back on my finger, and we held one another with a satisfying sense of comfort and peace. I quickly went to touch up my makeup, then we left to enjoy a wonderful celebration dinner which included our fresh tears containing more joy than pain regarding this special moment.

At our engagement dinner, Clinton and I agreed we had no intention of "renewing" our wedding vows. Though in the sight of the law, we never separated or pursued divorce, the two of us needed completely fresh vows to reflect walking into a new covenant together. We would not take this endeavor lightly. These vows needed to represent the various lessons God was teaching us. In the six weeks since Disclosure, the Lord led us through our very own "premarital counseling" which focused on many relational skills we desperately lacked in our first thirty years together.

We also acknowledged that both of us were ready for this next important step, and we didn't need an extended engagement. A decision had been made: Clinton proposed a new covenant with me, and I accepted. We were on the same page and the two of us desired to move forward in unity. At the same time, I was keenly aware of another aspect of our relationship that needed to be addressed: physical intimacy. The existence of Clinton's history with Sexual Addiction and infidelity *demanded* we approach this area of our lives with patience, care, and a new healthy perspective. Because our original wedding vows were broken, Biblically speaking, the two of us were no longer married. Sex was off the table. In fact, there was no changing in front of one another or showering while the other was in the bathroom. We slept beside each other, but both of us remained clothed to protect our purity. We needed to enter a new covenant *before* repair in our sexual relationship could begin. My heart slowly opened toward Clinton, and physical affection was increasing, but we chose to wait for any sexual expression until we were married again. Though my heart was ready to be bound to Clinton's once more, it didn't mean I was prepared for the "honeymoon" just yet. That part of our relationship required more time to heal first.

We set the date of our new wedding vows for July 1, 2024 - exactly seven weeks after Disclosure. Something felt right about the number that represented completion, healing, and promises fulfilled in the Bible. With limited time until our special day, we set to the work of writing new vows. It was imperative that we included pledging our unity, faithfulness, Christlike leadership and submission, being H.O.T. with one another, living in the Light, and honoring God's guidance by His Spirit and through the Word. We would commit to a *new* life together. Monday, July 1st, Clinton and I prepared our hearts and minds for what was about to take place. Once again, we got dressed up to commemorate this exceedingly special step in our journey. We decided to speak our vows and enter our new covenant together in the Art Room - the exact location of tremendous difficulty, grief, and pain would now become the site of joyful reconnection. We stood in that precious room, worshipping together to CeCe Winan's "Goodness of God," the same pivotal song from the drive to our Disclosure. Our melodies and tears flowed freely before the One who faithfully held our story all along the way. We didn't realize it until later that though dressed up, both of us stood barefoot on the carpet. We were on *Holy Ground*.

When the song ended, Clinton held my hands and asked Jesus to be in our midst as we joined our lives together once again. Then, he looked lovingly into my eyes as he proclaimed his new vows to me. Each phrase was spoken with purpose and tender care. He took his time, and I believed every word he uttered. As he finished, we both smiled through freely flowing tears. Then it was my turn. I looked up at the man before me, this *new man* God had been transforming daily. I spoke my heartfelt wedding vows to Clinton, mirroring the promises he just made to me. When I finished, we smiled and shared a tender kiss. I was my Beloved's, and he was mine. The two of us embraced for a long time, then expressed our deep gratitude to God for turning the page to a fresh chapter in our story.

Your Turn:

1. Work together to make a list of 5-10 of your most common spiritual disciplines (ex: prayer, fasting, serving others, etc.). Then, talk about what it might look like to encounter them with the attitude of *"Do with, not for."* Discuss how each of you could approach these valuable disciplines while participating *with* Jesus and not just checking the items off your list of Christian duties.

2. Separately, schedule a time to talk with a friend or small group of friends about what it means to be yoked with Jesus according to Matthew 11:28-30. Then, plan a time to share your discoveries with your spouse.

3. Read Ephesians 5:22-33 together. This passage describes the beautiful dance of leadership and submission in marriage as God designed. Wives, make a list of 10 things your husband could say or do to help you feel safe and covered in your relationship. Be sure to include physical, relational, and spiritual items. Husbands, make a list of 10 things your wife could say or do to help you feel appreciated as you care for and lead her. Each of you choose 2-3 items from your spouse's list and make an effort to practice them in the coming week. The following week, try a few different items from each list. At some point soon, discuss your findings of what is working well and what might need to be tweaked.

CHAPTER FOURTEEN: THE TRIP OF A LIFETIME

"For the beauty of the earth, for the glory of the skies
For the love which from our birth over and around us lies
Lord of all, to Thee we raise this our hymn of grateful praise"
~ Lyrics from the hymn "For the Beauty of the Earth"
by Folliot S. Pierpoint[1]

July 2024 can only be described as a month of expedited growth, healing, and repair. I (Clinton) felt extremely humbled by the Lord's obvious hand in our progress forward. The two of us were working diligently on ourselves and our coupleship, and from what I saw and heard in my recovery materials, we were defying the odds.

Months before Disclosure in May, Nikki and I decided to consider an extended vacation to celebrate our 30th anniversary. We wanted to plan thirty days away to commemorate our thirty years of marriage. In 2020, the two of us began traveling more. Covid stunted our original vacation plans that year as air travel became complicated, so in our spare time we built a teardrop style camper together. We thought it would be fun to visit the U.S. National Parks, so in September 2020, we pulled the new custom camper we affectionately named "Sparky" behind our Jeep Wrangler and set out for adventure! We made a large loop and saw 7 parks in 18 days! Over the course of the next few years, Nikki and I made several more trips and by 2024, we'd seen 32 of the 63 National Parks together.

In February 2024, I (Nikki) asked Clinton to seek the Lord with me about our big 30th anniversary trip. We agreed to take time separately to pray, then connect again at a later date to discuss God's wisdom and direction. With a trip of this size in the heavy tourist season late July, we had to make plans early or accommodations would be full. I prayed the very same day of my conversation with Clinton and immediately heard God's words of blessing over our special trip that summer. I wrote the Father's loving message in my journal, then waited for either my husband's confirmation or further direction from the Lord. At that time, Clinton was still in a delicate place in his repair with Jesus, so several days went by and I didn't hear anything regarding him seeking the Lord concerning our trip. After about a week, I gently inquired if he'd heard anything, and he responded that he hadn't prayed about it yet. I reminded him we needed to make plans sooner than later if we were going in July, so Clinton committed to listening for an answer that day. In the evening, he confirmed what I'd already heard about the Lord giving His blessing for us to go. We quickly secured accommodations for our adventure later that summer, and both of us were ecstatic!

Fast forward to May when our marriage blew up... We were focused on picking up the pieces for quite some time, so it didn't hit me until July: What about our trip? We were supposed to leave on July 26th, and an excursion of that size required at least a week of packing and preparation. I panicked a bit and wondered, are we even ready for something like this? Should we cancel? I was afraid to go on vacation, acting like my life hadn't just completely shattered due to my husband's infidelity.

I brought my concerns to Clinton, and my wonderful husband had the perfect answer. He said, "Why don't we ask Jesus?" He led me to our Conversation Chairs, and we sat facing one another. Clinton and I both took a few deep breaths, then got quiet before the Lord. After a few moments, we opened our eyes and looked at one another with smiles of delight. God spoke to us that He wasn't a bit surprised by the last few months, and when He said YES to our idea in February, He knew what was about to happen. My heart settled. I had a hopeful feeling this trip would be just what we needed, at just the right time.

As we prepped our belongings, we also prepared our hearts. Clinton and I met with Kyle to discuss the trip and healthy expectations, considering our current state of recovery. I was still unsure about sexual repair at that point, so Kyle suggested a book called *The Couples Guide to Intimacy* which spoke specifically to restoration after infidelity.[2] Clinton and I slowly began to work through the book in the weeks before our trip. I tend to be quite methodical, so I looked ahead in the book to see where we might be in the process while on our trip. I grew apprehensive and anxious, so we planned one more session with Kyle two days before leaving for our adventure. I shared my concerns about our road back to physical intimacy, and his response contained comforting wisdom. Kyle encouraged us that this book was full of great suggestions and practices; however, we needed to let the program work for us and not the other way around. I recognized my intense rule-follower mindset was getting in the way of being able to naturally experience growing intimacy as my heart, mind, and body were ready for it. Kyle mentioned if I felt open to "skipping ahead" in our intimacy journey while we were away, that was totally ok. When we returned, if I needed to back up to an earlier section of the process, that was fine too. This part of our healing required open and vulnerable communication, while paying close attention to my readiness for sexual repair.

Our thirty-day excursion encompassed extended time in our beloved Glacier National Park in Montana, our favorite park to date. We'd been there previously on five separate occasions, and I (Clinton) anticipated more grand adventures on this visit as well. After Glacier, we would drive north into Alberta, Canada to visit Waterton National Park, another wonderful repeat for us. Then, it was on to Banff, Yoho, and Kootenay National Parks, all new locations to explore. We packed up our Jeep Rubicon with two single kayaks on top and pulled a Jeep off-road camper trailer behind. On big trips like this, we enjoyed a combination of camping, boondocking, and a few nights in hotels or lodges. Early morning on July 26th, we pulled out of the driveway for a month on the road together. Our excitement was palpable!

We planned four days to drive from our home in North Carolina to the east side of Glacier National Park, with several fun stops along the way including "The Corn Palace." Located in *Mitchell,* South Dakota, it was obvious we had to check it out! Then, a problem happened... On day three of driving, Nikki landed in the "Anger" stage of the grief cycle, and she had very little to say to me... My past poor choices were top of mind for her that day and into the next morning. My wife struggled to express her feelings, so she mostly remained quiet. Mid-morning on day four of our trip, I was driving into Browning, Montana where you can just start to see the glorious Rocky Mountains for the first time. It was drizzling a bit and the weather matched Nikki's mood. She'd been silently looking out her window for quite some time. Then, I spotted a sight in front of us that I knew she needed to see. I carefully nudged her arm to get her attention, then nodded for her to look ahead...

I (Nikki) stared out the windshield at the widest and most vibrant rainbow I'd ever seen in my entire life! Right there in front of me, with my beloved Rocky Mountains as a backdrop, was God's promise of faithfulness. The Lord understood the questions in my heart: *WHY* did He let this happen to me? How could God truly love me and still allow my husband's unfaithfulness? Then, this rainbow. I believed it was my Heavenly Father's sweet promise for me in that fragile moment. I heard

His still, small voice say, "I've got you, Precious One. I know you don't comprehend My ways, yet I've had a plan all along and I'll never let you go." I wept as I gazed at that rainbow, and Clinton reached over with a sort of knowing, gently placing his hand on my leg. We rounded a bend to the left and Montana's nickname "Big Sky Country" became utterly apparent! The brilliant rainbow unfolded as a fully vibrant arch extending from one horizon to the other, while a faint double rainbow echoed above. I thought, "Ok Lord, I get the picture." Tears continued to flow, yet relief flooded my heart as I accepted the truth: One day I would truly be healed.

Our time in Glacier was filled with beauty, wonder, and the evidence of the Lord's presence at every turn. I (Clinton) had been inching toward Jesus, and the majesty of this place drew me even closer, like a moth to the flame. Because we'd been here many times before, Nikki and I both had our favorite places in the park. Nikki loved a certain spot in the eastern portion of Glacier, overlooking the "Two Medicine" valley. On many occasions, we took our camp chairs up the hillside and gazed at the gorgeous lake with jagged peaks in the background. My favorite spot lived on the western side of the park, as far north as you can travel by vehicle on a remote gravel road. This amazing place is called "Kintla Lake" and I've never experienced anything like it. Two Medicine Hill and Kintla Lake were the top two places Nikki and I envisioned when we spent time with Jesus. In our Conversation Chairs back home, we communed with Jesus (in our mind's eye) in these two special spots during prayer, worship, and even Immanuel Journaling. Now on our trip, we found ourselves in the actual locations, taking in the wonder with all our senses! It made these two spots even more precious to us (see photos).

Two Medicine Valley in Glacier National Park, Montana

Kintla Lake in Glacier National Park, Montana

The "One Minute Pause" app we mentioned previously introduced the two of us to the practice of being *with* Jesus. Previously, as we prayed or worshipped the Lord, we spoke and listened for His voice, but it was auditory only. John Eldridge encouraged us, through the "30 Days to Resilient" program on this app,[3] to spend time with Jesus in a visual sense. Nikki and I learned to close our eyes during prayer, worship, or simple quiet time with the Lord, and imagine being *with* Jesus in these beautiful places we love so dearly. We see His face shining on us with joy. We envision His responses and interactions with us. It has revolutionized the time we spend with the Lord! (We'll expound on this precious practice later in the book, so stay tuned.)

Throughout our thirty-day trip, I (Nikki) experienced a new level of Immanuel Journaling with Clinton. Sitting side by side in our camp chairs with glorious views of God's amazing creation brought a depth to our encounters with Jesus. Something about being in nature positioned the two of us with greater sensitivity to our Creator. We wrote Immanuel Journal entries daily, reading the precious words to one another, often through tears of joy. In one particular session, the Lord spoke to my heart about Clinton's journey with Him. God said of my husband, "He resisted, but I AM Irresistible!" It impacted me significantly to see and hear Clinton's relationship with Jesus repairing and deepening. The Lord was doing a mighty healing work in the two of us. While we were away, our Immanuel Journaling shifted from Interactive Gratitude to more of a conversational tone between each of us and Jesus. He spoke words of love and affection over us, as well as beautiful wisdom and direction for our healing journey moving forward, including physical intimacy. My feelings of safety and trust for Clinton were growing, and physical desire for my husband was returning. The Lord graciously met us on that trip, and He provided a beautiful start to a new sexual journey toward freedom and wholeness.

Over the course of our time in Montana and Canada, God displayed His attentive care over us. Clinton and I witnessed numerous ways the Lord made Himself known, specifically through the weather.

For example, the forecast for our week in Banff predicted rain every single day. In moments when the two of us needed rest, we were lulled to sleep by the sound of raindrops on our canvas camper top. Then, we'd get up to go on an adventure, the skies would clear, and the sun shined brightly! On another occasion, we planned to kayak, but the wind caused white-capped swells on the lake. By the time we arrived at our location, the waters calmed and produced a magical mirrored reflection of the glorious mountains! These things happened over and over again throughout our trip, and we knew God's goodness and mercy was following us all along the way. After a while, it became strangely predictable. We'd hike to a lake shrouded with low clouds and as soon as we stood on the shore, the clouds dissipated to reveal blue skies and crystal clear water, as still as glass. We could recount multiple times the Lord painted the sky before our eyes in magnificent sunrises and sunsets. One extravagant sunset on Two Medicine Hill remains an experience we will never forget! God made ways before us, not only with the weather. We were able to do several spontaneous activities that only occurred because of the Father's kind provision. These are all special memories of His faithfulness that we treasure to this day.

One such memory inspired the title of this book. Clinton and I were in Waterton National Park, and it was an especially tumultuous day for me emotionally. I struggled with Clinton's past choices and how to make sense of them as we walked forward. We were driving on a beautiful road through the park when I asked him to pull over. He found a spot and we sat in the vehicle as I openly revealed and processed my burdensome emotions. Clinton was right there by my side, empathizing with the havoc his actions caused. As I cried, he once again offered a heartfelt apology for the agony he inflicted on me. We stepped out of the Jeep, stood on the side of the road with the beautiful mountains as a backdrop, and grieved once again in a tearful embrace. As we quieted, I felt better, and we made our way to another scenic road nearby. This particular area of the park had been ravaged by a wildfire a few years prior. As far as the eye could see, dead trees with charred bark peppered the hillsides. At ground level, baby pine trees painted the earth a vivid green. Amidst the tiny trees were thousands of glorious purple wildflowers, a cacophony of color! We learned these plants are called "Fireweed" and they are the first things to spring up after a devastating forest fire. We found a spot to pull over and appreciate the magnificent sight. Clinton and I immediately realized God was revealing this incredible scene as a depiction of our story - the exact event that caused utter destruction in our marriage would also be the catalyst for *beautiful new life*. Fresh emotion surfaced for both of us at the gravity of this truth, and we retrieved our camera to capture the moment. Clinton's photograph became the cover art for this book meant to tell our story, *Glory From the Ashes*.

We want to be clear that our story is not one describing "*beauty from the ashes*" - how things burned to ash in our marriage and now they're beautiful. That version feels like the beauty is somehow connected to us; depicting what *we* did to successfully come back from the devastation. We purposefully chose the phrase *Glory From the Ashes* to communicate that it is God and God alone who receives the honor and praise in our story. Psalm 115:1 declares, "Not to us, Oh Lord, not to us, but to Your name give glory, for the sake of Your steadfast love and Your faithfulness!"

Your Turn:

1. When Nikki saw the massive vibrant rainbow in the Montana sky, she was reminded of God's faithfulness toward her. Looking back, where can you recognize God's faithful hand in your own lives? How has He come through in your family of origin, in your marriage, in your finances, in your children's lives, etc. Take some time to speak back and forth with your spouse remembering moments of God's faithfulness.

2. Have you been practicing Immanuel Journaling with your spouse through Interactive Gratitude? We sure hope so! Now, we'll add another layer to this intimate practice. Shift to a more conversational tone with Jesus. You can do it one of two ways: Either write back and forth with Him as you go along, or you can write all your personal thoughts and feelings on the paper first, then write how you sense Jesus responding back to you. Finish by enjoying the closeness of reading your entries aloud with one another.

3. Is there an area of your marriage that seems to resemble a forest destroyed by fire? Remain close to Jesus and be sure to pay close attention to signs of Glory He will cause to rise up from the ashes. Can you recognize any beautiful "Fireweed" springing to life in your story?

CHAPTER FIFTEEN: INTIMACY – LET'S GET DOWN TO BUSINESS

"I am my beloved's and my beloved is mine…" Song of Songs 6:3 (NIV)

In a book on marriage, you probably have an immediate thought regarding where we're headed with the word *Intimacy*. Yes, sex is a wonderful part of this concept, AND we aim to broaden the view to include so much more! Our approach is holistic in nature. We urge you to stand back with us and take in the many facets of intimacy available for exploration as a couple. This includes things like emotional, intellectual, spiritual, relational, and of course, physical intimacy. In our personal story, we both had a multitude of misconceptions and misunderstandings when it came to connecting on a deeper level, across the board. We encourage you to openly investigate where you could also be missing one another in this important area.

Prior to engaging in any variety of intimacy, we have learned to consider three helpful questions to make the process more fruitful and enjoyable:

1. Am I present?
2. Am I acting like myself?
3. Are my Relational Circuits (RC's) on?

First, what does it mean to be present? We realize this question may seem elementary but take a moment for some honest assessment. Do you ever approach your spouse already anticipating they will react as they have in the past? Maybe you carry relational pain from an unresolved conflict forward into the present. Or perhaps concerned about an issue in the future, your mind keeps drifting ahead. It could even be something as simple as distraction from the circumstances around you. Many different scenarios like these can prevent you from being fully present with your spouse. During our recovery, I (Nikki) regularly found my mind smack in the middle of the years long ago when Clinton's affair was active. My thoughts, words, and actions were drastically affected by my feelings about his past. Clinton may have been approaching me in the present, but even though my body was accounted for, my heart and mind were *not* in the here and now. For our circumstances, I required a tool to help me return to the present. My therapist, Monica, suggested that in the moments my brain looped back to the past, I needed to remind myself of who my husband is *now*. As I learned to speak the truth about Clinton's new choices and I returned to safety, I was able to reconnect to my husband in the present. "Now" is necessary to enjoy any form of intimacy.

Second, what does it mean to act like myself? In Chris Coursey's book *Transforming Fellowship,* he expounds on the relational skill of being able to "Act Like Myself" when experiencing difficult emotions.[1] We've also learned through our story that it's vital to live genuinely in all our interactions, especially when we desire to connect intimately. Each of us has been created in the image of God, and as such, our true identity is intended to reflect His likeness. For example, when I (Clinton) am living authentically from my core values, as opposed to wearing masks or operating out of lies of the enemy, I am acting like myself. I spent most of my life acting like what I perceived would be acceptable. Coming clean about my past provided an opportunity for me to practice living in my true identity for the very first time. I say "practice" intentionally, because after 49 years of living one way, it has required consistent practice to be *myself*. For example, a few months after Disclosure, Nikki came out to the shop and asked if I'd called a particular client to secure information we needed for their project. I answered yes, that I left a message, and was waiting for their reply. The truth was I actually *did not* call the customer, but I didn't want to face my wife's possible reaction to my forgetting. (I assumed she would react as she did in the past, and I overlooked that she could respond out of health in the present.) Nikki received my answer without question and went into the house. When I finished working for the day, I humbly approached my wife and confessed that I lied to her earlier. I relayed that I didn't want to be that *old* man anymore who covered the truth and hid my actions, and I asked her to forgive me. I conveyed to Nikki that I desire to act like myself in every situation, seen or unseen., and she kindly forgave me. Authenticity is another crucial prerequisite as we approach intimacy with our spouse.

Finally, we need to consider our Relational Circuits (RC's) before coming together in any type of intimacy. We previously explained this important topic in Chapter Ten, but we'll provide a quick reminder of the acronym C.A.K.E.[2] As you move toward your spouse for intimate connection, along with considering if you are present and acting like yourself, make sure your RC's are in the "on" position. Ask yourself the following:

1. Can I approach my spouse with Curiosity?
2. Am I able to Appreciate my spouse and their perspective?
3. Will I treat my spouse with Kindness?
4. Can I hold loving Eye Contact with my spouse?

I (Nikki) remember several Art Room Conversations in the weeks after Disclosure where I sensed my RC's flickering, or sometimes turning off completely, in the middle of an interaction with Clinton. I felt myself shut down or even go numb. When I recognized it, I asked for a moment to pause our discussion, so I could authentically reconnect. Sometimes, we don't even notice our RC's going offline. This could be an opportunity for the other spouse to gently step in with a suggestion such as, "It seems like something shifted, and I'm not feeling as connected to you right now. Would you be open to taking a moment to try and reconnect with me?" Always keep in mind, connection is the heart blood of any type of intimacy.

So, now you're both feeling present, acting like yourselves, and your RC's are on. It's time for an intimate encounter! As you approach one another, we remind you that being known is always a two-way street. As we shared in Chapter Five regarding our time in sex therapy, I (Clinton) now understand that Nikki opening up and vulnerably laying her heart before me wasn't enough to create the intimacy she truly desired. I was still withholding myself in this area, so it wasn't actually possible for my wife to be known as she longed to be. Revealing alone does not equal intimacy. Let me explain further using a simple science analogy. Suppose Nikki is baking soda. If she wanted to be "known," she could begin revealing all the different properties about herself. Nikki relays that she's a white powdered substance with a chemical makeup called sodium bicarbonate. She is alkaline and has a taste that's slightly salty. She can be used as a raising agent in yummy baked goods. She unveils "all the things" about herself. But as we said prior, Nikki won't encounter intimacy and the joy of being known unless I *interact* with her. Now, imagine I am vinegar (I know, probably not too difficult). I could describe myself as a clear liquid with an acidic property. I have a taste that is quite sharp and sour. I can also be used as a cleaning agent. I unfold various informative facts about myself to my wife, but that doesn't automatically result in intimacy or being deeply known. Here's where it gets interesting. At some point, you've most likely witnessed the result of combining baking soda and vinegar together. The simple white powder and sour liquid mix to create a foaming, expanding, bubbling concoction that's now a completely different substance! You see, Nikki couldn't fully open herself to me *until* I offered parts of myself that uncovered potential in her that she didn't even know existed. This is the beautiful picture of intimacy - the intermingling of our knowing and being known.

We also need to consider the balance of each spouse's offering. If Nikki brought a large container of her baking soda to the table and I only contributed a teaspoon of my vinegar, as the two of us combined, the results might be underwhelming. We're not trying to convey that each of you must share exactly equal parts of yourselves to create the ideal intimate encounter. We're all human. Our energy, capacity, and desire for connection naturally ebb and flow over time, even within the same day. As with the reaction between baking soda and vinegar, it's more about having the right proportions of each to create something interesting. Think back to a time when you felt particularly close to your spouse. Maybe you enjoyed a quiet walk in the woods or an engaging conversation. Perhaps you connected over a special time of prayer together or even shared an especially passionate kiss. I'd venture to guess you each brought just the right amount of yourself to the table to result in the "fizzy reaction" that made that encounter memorable.

It's also important to understand that every type of intimacy requires more than a single occasion of offering ourselves. Over time, a layering effect occurs that Nikki and I refer to as the "volley" of knowing one another. Let's suppose Nikki wants me to understand her in a new way. In order to be further known by me, she must choose to open up and reveal this part of herself. She has volleyed to me, so to speak. I receive what she's offered to me and respond by volleying back to her with my love and appreciation. Nikki will hopefully feel seen and heard through this exchange. As a result, she may desire to unveil more of herself so I can know her even more deeply. It doesn't have to happen immediately, but at some point, I will need to initiate a volley to Nikki, revealing another piece of myself to her. This process of knowing one another more intimately will ideally go back and forth, layer upon layer, building trust, safety, love, and affection over time. And... Sometimes we just don't get it right. Our spouse offers a volley, and we let the ball drop. It's not the end of the world. In our journey, Nikki and I have learned that a little humility, repentance, and reconnection goes a long way.

When done right, we've found that this volleying back and forth to know one another more deeply cultivates a strong and unifying intimacy. This is the Oneness all of us long for in marriage. Imagine the two sides of a zipper. One represents you, and the other, your spouse. As you come together, each individual tooth signifies an encounter of revealing yourselves to one another. Tooth upon tooth, you can connect, build, and grow together over time.

This exact same volley of knowing and being known happens in our relationship with the Lord as well. The great news is that His side of the encounter remains ever perfect; no worry of Him ever dropping the ball. It might look something like this: God reveals a facet of Himself, and I (Nikki) receive His volley. I see, hear, and know Him in a deeper way as a result. Then, I respond to Him with a volley of love and appreciation for what He's shown me. He, in turn, accepts my worship and offers yet another part of Himself back to me. This volley of knowing and being known continues between the two of us in His perfect timing and ways. Now, maybe even more intimate, in my opinion, is when the opposite transpires. I humbly choose to reveal a part of myself to the Lord, maybe something I'm not so proud to expose. My loving Father sees, hears, and knows me, just as I am. (Let me be clear, God knows me whether I choose to open myself to Him or not. At the same time, we're trying to convey the importance of experiencing the Lord's *response* to my openness.) He accepts the offering I've presented with perfect love, forgiveness, and acceptance, despite my imperfections. I receive the Lord's knowing of me, and the experience deepens my intimacy with Him. This creates safety and trust to reveal myself over and over again. Knowing and being known, what joy!

At this point in our journey, we felt the Lord nudging us to be known in another profound way - sharing our story with others. Clinton and I understood the importance of bearing one another's burdens through our journey thus far, and we agreed it was time to expand the circle. Clinton was living openly before Pete as well as his Pure Desire group, including several men he walked with in authentic accountability. I had several women in my "Betrayal and Beyond" group, along with the dear friends in my Identity Group. We both appreciated such support and encouragement in our recovery process, but no one in our personal sphere knew what the two of us were going through. Clinton and I spent time praying and discussing it, then came up with a short list of a few trusted people we believed could help "hold our story." Neither of us were ready to have our news spread yet, so we needed to feel safe that the folks we chose would keep this difficult information in complete confidence. We settled on the list and made plans to open our lives to these individuals. Each time we contacted people to schedule a meeting, we relayed there was something very heavy we wanted to share and asked if they had the capacity to hold it with us. We didn't want to assume in any way, so we gave them the opportunity to consider what we were asking. Every person on our list answered yes with gladness. Each time we prepared to unfold our story, questions loomed in my mind: Will these people judge Clinton harshly? Will they consider me a complete fool for "not knowing" about his affair all these years? Will they ever receive from us again spiritually once they hear the truth about our marriage? Over the summer months of 2024, we vulnerably revealed our shattering reality to those on our list. We were met time and time again with love, acceptance, and Christlike tenderness to our weakness. We were humbled over and over by God's glorious display of kindness through these precious people.

Then, the time came to openly share with our adult children. We invited our daughter, our son, and his wife to our home and spoke the truth to them as well. It wasn't easy, and the processing continues for all five of us, but we know God is in the middle of it all. Clinton and I believe we are breaking longstanding strongholds, and our choice to expose the darkness will provide opportunity for our children and our children's children for generations to walk in freedom as well! Each time we share our story, we include 1 John 1:5-7 which says, "God is light, and in Him is no darkness at all. If we say we have fellowship with Him while we walk in darkness, we lie and do not practice the truth. But if we walk in the light, as He is in the light, we have fellowship with one another, and the blood of Jesus His Son cleanses us from all sin." We have chosen to be known intimately as we walk in the Light! Will you choose the same?

Your Turn:

1. We've discussed how intimacy can be expressed in a variety of ways. In the case of physical intimacy in marriage, it may be difficult to see past the obvious form of sexual expression. Work together to create a list of as many ways you can think of to experience physical intimacy together, without it alluding to or leading to sex. As a wife, which are your favorites? As a husband, what do you prefer? Now, share some non-sexual physical affection with one another. Have fun!

2. In Chapter Three, we asked you to consider what dysfunctions might have been present early in your marriage and if they are still hanging around in the background. First, take a few moments separately to gather your thoughts on this. Then, practice approaching the intimate conversation by checking to see if you are present, able to act like yourself, and if your RC's are on (think C.A.K.E.). When you're both ready, discuss any dysfunctions that need to be addressed, as well as one action step to move toward a healthier way of relating. (Practice Active Listening and be open to outside help if you get stuck.)

3. Remember the "volley" of knowing and being known? Now it's time to practice. Spouse #1, reveal something from your recent past that brought you joy. Explain why it did so, and how it made you feel. Spouse #2, genuinely thank your mate for opening up to you, then share what emotions you felt while hearing your spouse's openness. Spouse #1, express what it was like to be seen, heard, and known in this way. Then, switch and begin the whole process again. (It's much easier to share situations that bring us joy rather than pain, so that's why we began there. Once you have the mechanics of the "volley" idea, try the concept with something a little more vulnerable, like a difficult moment from your childhood or a challenging circumstance you're facing at work.)

CHAPTER SIXTEEN: WHAT IS SPIRITUAL INTIMACY?

"As the deer pants for streams of water, so my soul pants for You, oh God... Deep calls to deep in the roar of your waterfalls; all Your waves and breakers have swept over me." Psalm 42:1,7

If we could only share one thing we've learned on the road to healing in our marriage, we wholeheartedly agree it would be the beautiful concept of Spiritual Intimacy. This was the missing piece neither of us knew was lacking, but that we both longed for in our deepest parts. Each of us experienced personal times of intimacy with Jesus throughout the years, yet somehow we failed to understand the indescribable joy of blending our closeness with Him and our closeness with one another. We recognize it sounds extremely simple, and you may think you already have the principle of Spiritual Intimacy down pat.

Maybe you do. We most certainly did not. The two of us spent time together over the years praying, reading the Word, attending church services as a family, worshipping with others, fasting, serving those around us… These valuable spiritual disciplines can foster intimacy, but are they actually bonding you to Jesus AND to your spouse *simultaneously*? Is your love and devotion to the Lord reflected in your marriage? Is your connection with Jesus impacting your relationship with your spouse in ever deepening affection? We long to share and impart what we've experienced on our road to Spiritual Intimacy.

When I (Clinton) heard the Lord speak to me about Covering and how to lovingly lead my wife, you'll recall He revealed a powerful phrase that broadened my view of relating with Him: *Do with, not for.* This shifted the many spiritual disciplines listed above from my unfortunate sense of duty, obligation, or performance to meaningful encounters *with* Jesus. After Disclosure, Nikki and I quickly began to understand that our connection to the Lord *while connecting to each other* was vital to our healing process. Now, we have an even more profound understanding that this attachment between Jesus and one another is imperative throughout our marriage, not just in the restoration after something difficult. We see this truth pictured beautifully in Ecclesiastes 4:12 where the writer says, "A cord of three strands is not quickly broken." (NIV) I challenge you to think of this imagery beyond a simple "braided" cord made up of you, your spouse, and the Lord. Imagine that the first strand represents your life as you weave yourself together with God (Father, Son, and Spirit). The second strand symbolizes your spouse, purposefully interlacing themselves with the Trinity. The third strand signifies the two of you in Oneness through the covenant of marriage, as you simultaneously knit yourselves together with the triune God. Finally, these three distinct strands, already individually reinforced through connection to the Lord, now intertwine to create this *cord* that cannot be quickly broken! I have come to understand that this interwoven three-way bond between me, my God, and my spouse is a depiction of strength, safety, and joy that words fail to properly express!

So, back to the concept of *Do with, not for*. How do we spend time *with* Jesus? Nikki and I would love to share a simple activity that helped set a foundation for the two of us, then we'll build upon it. Remember back to our favorite spots in Glacier National Park and how we began spending time with Jesus there in our mind's eye when back at home? We hope you took the time to try this out for yourselves in the exercises at the end of Chapter Fourteen. We'll take a moment here to quickly review, in case you need a refresher.

We imagine every one of you has a particular place you've visited that you remember with fondness. Perhaps you can easily call to mind a time sitting with your bare feet on a warm sandy beach, with the sound of the waves crashing on the shore as you enjoy the smell of the salty air. Maybe you remember an experience walking through a quiet forest surrounded by the fresh scent of pine as you approach a dazzling waterfall, the cool mist landing on your skin. Any memory that stands out in your mind will work. Now, sit somewhere quiet with your mate, close your eyes for a few moments, and individually remember your own personal scene. (Nikki and I enjoy playing William Augusto's instrumental worship music softly in the background.) As you envision your beautiful setting, picture Jesus walking into it as He joins you there. Simply be *with* the Lord while enjoying your memory, in His presence. After you finish comes the very best part: *Share your encounter with your spouse*. What did you imagine? Relay the details of what you remember seeing, hearing, smelling... What did it feel like to invite Jesus into that special spot with you? Maybe it was wonderful, or maybe you struggled to stay focused, or you couldn't envision the Lord at all in that scene. Offer your authentic experience with your spouse, because this sets the stage for the intimacy we're after. Spending time with Jesus in your mind's eye might be completely foreign to you. You may have a brain like mine that struggles to stay focused on any one thing for very long. It might require practice to settle into being *with* Jesus, and maybe more so, opening up to share what occurred with your spouse. We highly encourage you to stay with it, because we're headed into some wonderfully rich territory as we continue on this path.

Once you are both regularly able to recall a special scene and invite Jesus to be with you in the midst of it, we'll add the second layer. This includes *interacting* with the Lord in your encounter. As you envision a memorable spot in your mind with Jesus (while your spouse imagines their own special place with Him), now think about how you'd like to relate with Jesus and how He might connect with you. Do you want to hold His hand or rest your head on His shoulder? Will He wrap you in a loving embrace or joyfully dance with you? What is the expression on His face? Can you sense His delight in being with you? Again, when you conclude your moments with Jesus, tell your spouse all you experienced. This vulnerability might feel uncomfortable for one or both of you. Remember the phrase "into-me-you-see" describing intimacy? Nikki and I found our connection ever deepening as we opened up to each other regarding our personal times with Jesus.

Are you ready for the third layer in this process? Once you practice being with the Lord in a special spot (which can be different each time, by the way) and envision interacting with Him, now open yourself in a new way. This time, consider what Jesus would like to *say* to you. What phrases will He speak over you as you interact with Him? I'll quickly revisit the encouragement we offered when introducing Interactive Gratitude as an Immanuel Journaling practice. How would a loving parent speak to their child? What kinds of things would dear friends say to each other? As long as the words you sense from Jesus line up with the Scriptures and His character found within the Bible, receive His words with joy! As an added comfort, when you speak about what you hear with your spouse, you have a sounding board to make sure your encounter reflects the Jesus we know from the Word of God. If something doesn't match up to the Lord's character, gently bring that to the light with your spouse and lovingly correct what might need realignment. When it's presented with kindness, we can consider the input as an opportunity to learn and grow together.

Finally, the fourth layer in this practice involves not only listening for what Jesus wants to say to you but actually *conversing* with Him as well.

Talk back and forth with the Lover of your soul! Offer your honest thoughts and feelings to Him and listen for how He might respond. Practice quieting yourself and wait for Jesus to share His own thoughts with you. Then, imagine how you would reply back to Him. The Lord desires a *relationship* with us. It goes back to the truth that intimacy is never one-sided. Remember the "volley" of knowing and being known? It applies to our marriage, it applies to our relationship with the Lord, AND it extends to sharing these spiritual interactions with Jesus in the presence of our spouse.

As the Lord unfolded this avenue to practice being with Him then openly share our encounters with each other, Spiritual Intimacy deepened between the two of us. I (Nikki) joined Clinton as we began applying this experience to other spiritual disciplines as well. For instance, one afternoon we sat in our Conversation Chairs praying together for several people in our lives. When we finished, Clinton told me how he loved imagining that he ushered each one before Jesus on the shores of Kintla Lake in Glacier National Park. A lightbulb went off for me in that moment: I never considered being *with* Jesus as I prayed, actually bringing others before Him in my mind! It completely changed my prayer life! Now when the two of us pray, it's no longer simply words spoken to the Lord, but we see His face as we talk with Him. We take time to visualize how He might interact with those we are praying for. What a lovely shift! Then, after we're done praying, Clinton and I talk about the experiences of our prayer time with each other. I have come to treasure these intimate moments with my husband.

We've applied the concept to worship as well. The two of us will enter a time of praise and worship, and I can see Jesus with me on Two Medicine Hill as I sing or bow or lift my hands in adoration before Him. Other times, I'm on the pebbled shore of Kintla Lake. I imagine the heavens open up to reveal God on the throne, Jesus at His right side, the Holy Spirit mingling all around me, and I sing with a host of angels as I bow before my great God! Each encounter with the Lord can be different, and Clinton and I openly share with each other the time we spent with Jesus, cultivating our Spiritual Intimacy.

Spending time with the Lord was also helpful as I sensed Him prompting me to continue my road to forgiveness. One evening several months after Disclosure, Clinton was attending his Pure Desire meeting, so I was home alone. I humbly chose obedience to the Lord's leading and journaled my thoughts and feelings about forgiving "the other woman." I knew it wouldn't be an easy task, and I asked Jesus to be *with* me in the process. With soft worship music in the background, I closed my eyes and envisioned a yellow Formica kitchen table and chairs, the 1950's style. Sitting quietly at the table, I asked Jesus to join me. He lovingly held my hand, and with a deep breath, I imagined Clinton's affair partner coming in and sitting across from me. The details of those moments are mine to hold, but I will say Jesus kindly helped me to begin releasing her from the many ways she personally hurt me and my marriage. I'd love to report that this single encounter completed my forgiveness journey toward her, but it wouldn't be the truth. I understand now that forgiveness is a *process*, a series of choices we make over time to release the pain, bitterness, and grief wrapped up in offenses committed against us. Forgiveness is a lifestyle that leads to freedom. When Clinton returned from his meeting, I openly shared with him about my special time of forgiveness in the presence of the Lord.

I also needed Jesus with me as I released and forgave Clinton. This important step actually occurred a few days before the two of us spoke our fresh vows and committed to a brand-new covenant together. That afternoon, I invited Clinton for a face-to-face meeting regarding my forgiveness. Before we met, I spent time alone detailing in my journal each separate offense Clinton committed against me through his years in Sexual Addiction, including the time spent in his affair. Then, as I sat facing Clinton in the Art Room, I once again imagined Jesus right there beside me. It was extremely healing to speak forgiveness to my husband, naming one specific offense after the other as I released them into the loving hands of my Savior. Clinton and I wept together throughout that vulnerable process. What a beautiful and freeing way to enter our *new* marriage just a few days later. We are so grateful to Jesus for being *with* us in those tender moments!

We've spoken several times about the important role Immanuel Journaling played in our road to wholeness. I (Clinton) want to expound on how this particular tool cultivated such profound Spiritual Intimacy between the two of us. Earlier in this book, we introduced the concept of Interactive Gratitude, journaling our thanksgiving to the Lord then writing His response to our grateful expression. Next, Nikki and I included not only gratitude, but also a conversational tone between ourselves and Jesus. Now, we encourage you to incorporate being *with* Jesus while you practice Immanuel Journaling. Envision yourself before Him as you pour out your thoughts and feelings on the paper. Then, pause to imagine seeing His face, His expression, His actions, and denote the non-verbal interactions along with the words Jesus speaks back to you. This visualization adds yet another depth to an already special practice.

Please hear me. The most important part of Immanuel Journaling, in our experience, is reading the entries to one another *out loud*. This is where Spiritual Intimacy has the chance to flourish! We've found this process provides a layered effect similar to the "volley" of knowing and being known that we talked about previously. First, each spouse encounters personal time relating to Jesus through journaling. This is a wonderful step with great merit all on its own, but we're just getting started! The benefits grow exponentially as we read aloud. I read the words on my journal page to Nikki, and my voice proclaims to my own ears the precious exchange that just occurred between me and my beloved Savior. That does something in my spirit! On top of that, I get to witness my wife's reaction to hearing my intimate conversation with Jesus. Often, she smiles, nods, agrees, or even sheds a tear regarding my exchange. After I finish reading, we switch so Nikki has the opportunity to experience the same joyful process as she reads her interaction with Jesus aloud to me. We've also noticed another wonderful byproduct of consistently sharing through Immanuel Journaling: I get to hear how my wife talks with Jesus and how He responds to her. I discover the phrases they choose and the intimate names they use with one another. She hears the same of my interactions with Jesus. We see facets of the Lord through the other person that may not have opened to us otherwise. This circles right back to the fact that we were fashioned as image bearers of God, created with the potential to reflect His character to those around us. In the practice of Immanuel Journaling with our spouse, we can mirror God's attributes back to our mate. Even more exciting is that as we grow together, we have the opportunity to display who our God is to the world around us, *through* our marriage! What a privilege and a joy to experience Spiritual Intimacy with both Jesus and my spouse!

Your Turn:

1. Where is your favorite spot in nature? If you close your eyes and remember it, what do you see, hear, feel, smell? Take a few moments to experience being *with* Jesus in that place utilizing one of the suggestions we offer in this chapter. Share what you encountered with your spouse, including how it made you feel.

2. Try visualizing being *with* the Lord as you pray for someone together with your spouse. Envision "presenting" that person to Jesus as you pray for them. Afterwards, discuss what that was like with your spouse.

3. Are you beginning to understand the concept of Spiritual Intimacy as it relates to your spouse? How would you describe it in your own words? Are you intentionally carving out time and space in your lives to connect with Jesus - together? If not, take a moment to schedule it on your calendar now!

CHAPTER SEVENTEEN: LIVING IN THE LIGHT

"I wanna be in the light as You are in the light
I wanna shine like the stars in the heavens
Oh, Lord, be my light and be my salvation
'Cause all I want is to be in the light
All I want is to be in the light"
~ Lyrics from DC Talk's remake of the song "In the Light" by Charlie Peacock[1]

As the two of us walked consistently in deeper connection with Jesus and each other, I (Clinton) began to understand how Spiritual Intimacy could extend outside of our marriage to include those around us. Nikki and I had both developed a circle of support, and the Lord began teaching us to share our personal interactions with Him in our relationships with those individuals. The process involves walking openly together in the Light.

September 2024, I saw the need to start another Pure Desire

group more centrally located for several of us attending a different group the year prior. The Lord provided a location, and this small group of men gathered for our initial weekly meeting of the new year. God had recently revealed a life-changing message to me, and I shared it for the first time that evening. At that gathering, I related the principles to Sexual Addiction, but I quickly realized this is an important truth for believers across the board. It all starts with a bus.

I love logic problems, and there's one that includes a drawing of a bus (see Figure 1).

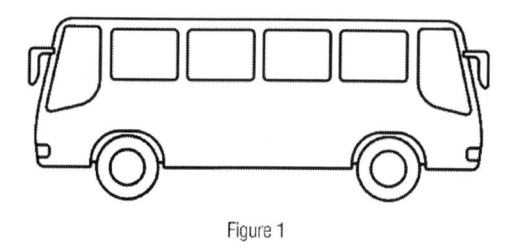

Figure 1

The front and back of the vehicle are perfectly mirrored to one another, including bumpers, windows, wheels, etc. The question is: Which way is the bus traveling? When the problem is presented, people often struggle, thinking they don't have enough information. In reality, they're focused on what they see, without considering what they don't see. A clue to help solve the problem is to ask, how do I get on the bus? When you recognize you don't see the door, you can conclude it's on the other side of this bus, therefore, the bus is traveling to the left.

You see, each of us is traveling on a journey. Imagine you are a stick figure in the middle of a page, with Jesus to the left and whatever sins you personally struggle with to the right (see Figure 2).

LIVING IN THE LIGHT

JESUS   🧍   SIN

Figure 2

I believe it's true that we all desire to protect ourselves from falling into sin, so we often try putting things between us and that potential problem to keep ourselves safe. For instance, we might utilize tools such as attending church meetings, reading scripture, walking in accountability, reaching out to friends, listening to podcasts or sermons, etc. (see Figure 3). Every one of these examples is good, right, and helpful.

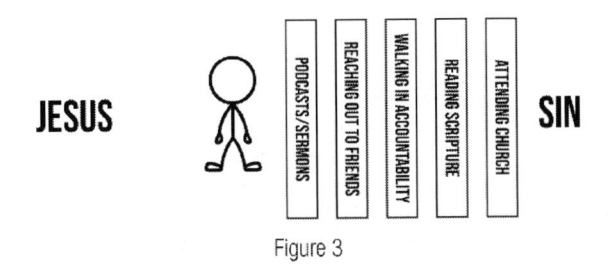

JESUS   🧍 | PODCASTS/SERMONS | REACHING OUT TO FRIENDS | WALKING IN ACCOUNTABILITY | READING SCRIPTURE | ATTENDING CHURCH | SIN

Figure 3

These tools can encourage, strengthen, and build our faith in the ways they minister to us. Now comes the real question to consider: Are these valuable practices simply keeping you away from your personal struggles, or are they propelling you toward Jesus? To answer this question, I refer you back to the bus illustration. *Which way are you facing?* Are you focused on using tools as safeguards to prevent behaviors that ultimately lead to sinful problems? Or are your eyes fixed on Jesus as these helpful tools propel you closer in your connection to Him? The key is to turn *toward* Jesus (see Figure 4).

137

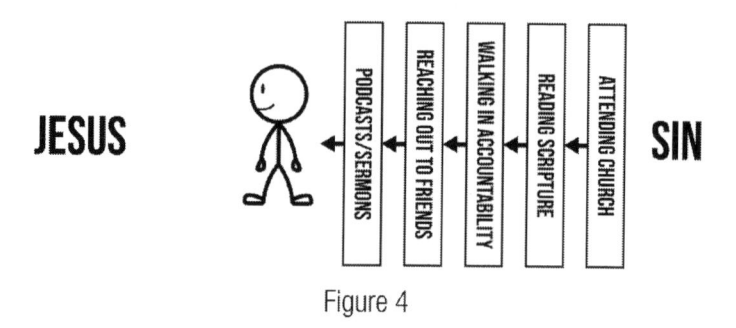

JESUS ← PODCASTS/SERMONS ← REACHING OUT TO FRIENDS ← WALKING IN ACCOUNTABILITY ← READING SCRIPTURE ← ATTENDING CHURCH ← SIN

Figure 4

I believe turning our attention *from* using tools to keep us from sinful behavior *to* focusing on Christ lies in the act of true confession. What do we mean by true confession? It requires humbling ourselves and admitting where we've missed the mark. We confess before God for the forgiveness of our sins, and I'd like to suggest according to James 5:16, we confess our sins before *each other* so we may be healed.[2] As followers of Jesus, we need to recognize sin not only according to the Ten Commandments, but also to the Sermon on the Mount. Jesus clearly communicated that sin is not in actions alone, but it involves the attitude of our heart as well. In Matthew 5:27-28 Jesus instructed, "You have heard that it was said, 'You shall not commit adultery.' But I say to you that everyone who looks at a woman with lustful intent has already committed adultery with her in his heart." Confessing visible sin that results from our choices seems obvious, but we must also practice confessing the unseen sin in our minds and hearts.

If we long to live in the Light, I believe our confession must encompass both sin *and* the temptation or "draw" toward sin. Let's be clear, temptation is not sin. Yet, if we do not bring temptations to the Light through true confession, they can act as a noose that eventually pulls us down a path of destruction. We see this progression clearly in James 1:14-15 which states, "But each person is tempted when he is lured and enticed by his own desire. Then desire when it has conceived gives birth to sin, and sin when it is fully grown brings forth death." Can you see how crucial it is to practice the confession of sin, *as well as* the draw that pulls us toward it? This is the purpose of growing something called a Confessional Community.³ In the years I struggled with Sexual Addiction, it seems obvious that I needed to confess my sins regarding infidelity. At the time, I wasn't even willing to do that. Now, imagine if long ago I had knit myself into a safe Confessional Community where I was truly open before other believers. If I practiced confessing my temptations and the draw pulling me *toward* destructive choices, I could have potentially avoided the resulting unfaithfulness all together.

Humbling ourselves to confess both sin and temptation before others is vulnerable work. It requires us to reveal ourselves in Honesty, Openness, and Transparency. We choose to be seen, heard, and known as we walk in the Light. This sounds a lot like Spiritual Intimacy, doesn't it? As we've been layering the concepts of practicing Spiritual Intimacy with your spouse, it's also important to expand your circle to include others. Please understand, we are NOT suggesting you go to your weekly Life Group meeting and air your "dirty laundry" just to get things off your chest. Confessional Community encompasses purposeful connection with others where Spiritual Intimacy can be cultivated. It might not be a group of people that is already established in your life. In fact, it most likely is not. For instance, my Confessional Community starts with my wife, then expands to my spiritual oversight, as well as two men I've walked in relationship with for many years, and a couple other men the Lord knit my heart together with from my Pure Desire group. These are the people I trust to receive my confessions, and I've given them access to approach me regarding those sins or temptations as well. It's also important to note that the people in my Confessional Community may or may not include me in their own Confessional Community. My community is for *me*. And your community will be for *you*. These become safe relationships where we confess our sins and receive healing. Furthermore, our Confessional Community is also where we confess our *draw* toward sin, so we can live freely in the Light.

I (Nikki) want to emphasize that this concept of being open before others is not reserved for those recovering from addictions or what people might deem as "horrific sins." Who needs Confessional Community? *Humans.* The human condition provides opportunity for sin and temptation, on a daily basis. Every one of us needs a safe place to authentically reveal our flaws. We do this before other flawed individuals, as well as a loving God who sees us all through the sacrifice of His precious Son. The beautiful fruit of Confessional Community lies in 1 John 1:7 which says, "But if we walk in the light, as He is in the light, we have fellowship with one another, and the blood of Jesus cleanses us from all sin." What freedom and joy!

The concept of Confessional Community encompasses so much more than simply opening up to others concerning our shortcomings. Clinton and I have included these circles as a place to expand and grow our experience of Spiritual Intimacy. Remember from the last chapter we described this type of intimacy as *simultaneously* blending closeness with Jesus and closeness with our spouse. We've learned to expand this same principle to other relationships as well. Over time, we began utilizing the tools that fostered Spiritual Intimacy in our marriage with those in our Confessional Communities. For example, we introduced the practice of Immanuel Journaling to several people in our close circles. We didn't simply explain how to do it. Instead, we invited them *in the moment* to try it with us, including reading our entries aloud to one another. We've come to treasure these special moments! Clinton and I also Share Joy with those in our Confessional Communities. Furthermore, we've had precious times of being *with* Jesus along with others, then we experienced the joy of vulnerably speaking about our encounters with one another. There are many different approaches and a multitude of tools that can be used to foster deeper Spiritual connection with those around you. Feel free to get creative! We're just scratching the surface of how Spiritual Intimacy can affect both your marriage and your personal communities!

Your Turn:

1. Tools are extremely valuable to help us steer clear of sinful choices, but when we focus on them exclusively, we tend to live in "behavior management" instead of true freedom. Like most people, you've probably experienced diligently avoiding a particular behavior, then inevitably falling back into the same old pattern. What is an area of your life where you see this cycle repeating over and over again? Have you been using tools (like accountability groups, prayer, podcasts, scripture, etc.) as a checklist to keep you away from sin? How could it look differently to use these things to propel you toward Jesus and focus on Him?

2. Confessional Community is not typically your men's breakfast group from church or your women's weekly Bible study. This type of community is made up of a few trusted individuals with whom you can build Spiritual Intimacy and be H.O.T. (Honest, Open, and Transparent). Husbands, with which men in your life can you build this type of relationship? Wives, what women can make up your safe place? Each of you take a step this week to begin developing your Confessional Community.

3. We discussed how living in the Light involves confessing both sin and the "draw" toward sin. Talk with your spouse about what thoughts and feelings this concept evokes in you. Are you willing to begin practicing the openness and vulnerability required to live in the Light before your Confessional Community, as well as your spouse? (Remember to use wisdom and seek support in the process if this level of honesty is a new experience in your marriage. Be open to professional assistance if needed.)

CHAPTER EIGHTEEN: NEW EVERY MORNING

"Forget the former things; do not dwell on the past. See, I am doing a new thing! Now it springs up; do you not perceive it? I am making a way in the wilderness and streams in the wasteland." Isaiah 43:18-19 (NIV)

    The story of our marriage began with a couple of naive kids, each carrying their own baggage full of lies leading to false identity, unrealistic expectations of sex and marriage, masks to hide true thoughts and feelings, and no tools to navigate the difficulties that would inevitably unfold. Despite all that was stacked against us, God demonstrated His grace and mercy toward us, over and over again. I (Clinton) recognize His display in countless ways throughout my history with Sexual Addiction. For instance, I can now see God's graceful hand as I look back over Nikki's multiple discoveries of my use of pornography early in our marriage. I acknowledge the Lord's merciful intervention in the form of phone records that exposed my extra-marital relationship. His wonderful grace and mercy were evident as my sexual struggles came back to light in September 2023. The tragedy in these grace-filled opportunities from the Lord is that instead of humbling myself, I chose pride every time. I hid my actions and lied about them, partitioning off parts of my heart from God, my wife, and others who cared about me.

In this area of my life, the Lord faithfully continued to extend His mercy and grace to me until I finally chose humility. Shortly after realizing a polygraph test would be part of my Disclosure, something shifted in my heart, and I chose to surrender to the Lord. I finally humbled myself before God and actually faced the sins I once vowed to keep secret. As I did this, my Heavenly Father ran to meet me, welcoming me home with open arms! This led to a process of my true repentance before Him, which extended out to Kyle, Pete, and a few other men in my circle.

At that point, God invited me to the NEW. He offered me the precious opportunity to ultimately be known more deeply by my wife. The Full Therapeutic Disclosure on May 13, 2024 marked my decision to answer YES to His invitation. I genuinely humbled myself before Nikki, revealing the whole truth of my past choices. I allowed her to see, hear, and know me completely for the first time in our three decades together.

I (Nikki) walked a similar road with the Lord. God extended his beautiful grace and mercy to me many different times in my life, including through the Disclosure of my husband's infidelity. At first glance, this excruciating situation might not seem full of the Lord's grace *or* mercy. The truth is I faced the exact same choice as Clinton, or anyone else for that matter. Would I respond to the Lord's plan with humility, or would I choose pride? From the outside looking in, you may argue I had every right to be furious, shocked, utterly devastated... Believe me, I was. But I made the difficult decision to humble myself before God and believe that in His sovereignty, He had a perfect plan for my life that somehow included *even this*. The Lord invited me to the NEW, just like he invited my husband. I chose to say YES to His invitation. Through circumstances I would *never* have asked for, God has been healing and redeeming my personal story, as well as Clinton's, and He gave us the beautiful opportunity to create a completely new marriage after thirty years.

Brand new relationships involve brand new people. I (Clinton) found that Disclosure created a line in the sand for the two of us, and we could never go back to the way things were before. Frankly, neither of us wanted to either. Nikki and I began to practice consistently being Honest, Open, and Transparent (H.O.T.) with each other every day. We opened our hearts and minds, vulnerably sharing the deepest parts of ourselves, hiding nothing. It felt wonderful to be authentically seen and heard, which led to our continued "volley" of knowing and being known more truly than ever before. We both learned how to live in the Light, regularly confessing sins as well as temptations with one another. For the first time in our marriage, Nikki and I began to understand the beautiful freedom that comes from the *process* of genuine forgiveness. All these NEW aspects of our relationship blended and created space for Spiritual Intimacy to flourish. God revealed His perfect design: That we might experience Oneness with each other, in the midst of beautiful Oneness with Him.

Practicing Spiritual Intimacy as husband and wife paved the way to enjoy the same vulnerable openness in our Confessional Communities as well. Nikki and I have each grown a circle around us where we not only confess our sins, but also the draw toward sin tempting us to walk in old patterns and past ways of thinking. Immense safety results for both of us as we choose to live in the Light alongside those around us.

This entire process leads to an amazing outcome: *Transformation*. Becoming new is an ongoing journey, day by day. I (Nikki) love the encouraging truth from Romans 12:2, "Do not conform to this world, but be transformed by the renewing of your mind..." Clinton and I have learned through this stretching season that renewing our minds takes consistent effort. Imagine your mind encompassing well established highways that developed over your lifetime, leading you to think, act, and respond in very specific ways. It happens without even knowing, because there is virtually no resistance while traveling down a highway. The challenging work of renewing your mind is more like moving through a dense forest that no person has ever traversed. First, you might need an axe to remove large trees and create a rough pathway. Then, you may have to wield a machete to clear brush and smaller plants. It's painstaking labor just to get the process started! Then, the hard work continues by using the path consistently over time to produce a distinguishable trail through the woods. If you neglect to utilize and maintain that path regularly, eventually the forest will reclaim the trail. As we renew our mind, we literally forge new pathways in our brain. The old highways don't magically disappear, but with practice, the fresh paths can become our *new* highways. This is such good news!

So, how do we go about renewing our minds? Clinton and I believe the key is found in Romans 8:5-6 which says, "For those who live according to the flesh set their minds on the things of the flesh, but those who live according to the Spirit set their minds on the things of the Spirit. For to set the mind on the flesh is death, but to set the mind on the Spirit is life and peace." As we regularly make the decision to occupy our mind with the things God intends, we begin living in the Light and the result is life and peace. God does the beautiful work of transforming our minds and making us NEW!

The two of us have found such hope in the truth of Lamentations 3:22-23, "The steadfast love of the Lord never ceases; His mercies never come to an end; they are new every morning; great is Your faithfulness." Every morning as we wake, God's tender mercies are brand new. His newness *never ends*. He provides an opportunity for each one of us to be made new, every single day. I walk a personal road of becoming new every morning. Clinton has his own journey to newness each day. As a result, our marriage is daily being made new as well. If you choose to engage the story of your marriage with Jesus, it's vital to understand that both you and your spouse must do the deep work leading to wholeness. When one or the other holds back, *growth will be stunted*. Even in various forms of addiction, the hurt or offended spouse can't simply sit back and wait for the struggler to "get their act together." Both husband and wife need to press into Transformation with the Lord individually in order to experience Transformation as a couple. Now, we ask: Are *you* ready to say YES to the Lord's invitation? Can you sense Him calling you deeper? Are you open to humbling yourself, submitting to His perfect design for your life and your marriage? Will you purposefully turn away from old patterns of thinking and relating, turn toward Jesus, and be made NEW in Him?

The story of our marriage is far from over, and we both still experience moments that hurt to remember. We steadfastly remain on this path toward freedom, healing, and wholeness in all areas of our marriage, and *there is hope*. The very circumstances that caused utter destruction in our relationship have become the grace-filled catalyst for our *Transformation*. To God alone be the honor and praise, and may He forever receive *Glory From the Ashes!*

As our time together draws to an end, we want to express our deep gratitude to each of you for choosing to read our story. We sincerely hope that unfolding the difficulties in our marriage, as well as our beautiful journey toward redemption, gives you the courage and hope to engage your own story with Jesus. Wherever you've been or wherever you are right now, this is our heartfelt prayer for you and your marriage:

Oh Lord, be magnified. Be exalted above all else. Your sovereign ways are higher than we can fathom, and we admit this hasn't been an easy story to tell. At the same time, the two of us are exceedingly grateful for the opportunity to walk this path and share our personal journey, for *Your great name's sake*. Not to us, but to You alone be the Glory!

Father, we bring each individual who has read our story before you now - every husband, every wife, those who deeply love one another and desire more of You, those who've forgotten why they fell in love and no longer sense Your presence, the broken and hurting, the people who are separated or divorced or even living separate lives under the same roof, the angry, the confused, the lonely, the ones wearing masks or believing lies of the enemy, the ones longing for something more in their marriage, and everything in between. Jesus, thank You for loving each one right where they are at this very moment.

Lord, we ask You to arrest each person by way of Your grace and mercy. Use whatever You see fit to capture their attention, even if these circumstances feel challenging, stretching, and extremely difficult. Enable each spouse to choose humility and surrender to Your ways, laying down selfish pride, Lord. We ask that You extend Your loving invitation to this husband and wife, the invitation to know and be known more deeply than ever before. Give each one the courage to say YES as You call them deeper into their own stories and the story of their marriage together.

Father, the two of us are still walking this road, and we link arms with each husband and wife as we all learn more of Your beautiful design for marriage. Holy Spirit, convict us when we are not honest. Spur us on in complete openness and encourage us to live transparently. Let this be a lifestyle that we pursue every day as we walk in the Light, with You and with one another. Reveal who we can connect with in safety and vulnerability to form our Confessional Communities. As we practice confessing our sins one to another, we pray that You heal us, Lord. Heal our minds, heal our hearts, and heal our bodies. Teach all of us to humbly confess the "draw" or temptation to sin in our Confessional Community, and in health and safety with our spouse. Expose the lies we've believed so we can live abundantly in Your perfect truth!

Lord, You've given the two of us a glimpse of Spiritual Intimacy, and we ask that You lavish on this couple the indescribable joy of blending their closeness with You and their closeness with one another. Jesus, invite this husband and wife into Oneness with each other in the midst of beautiful Oneness with You. Give this couple the courage to say YES to your invitation. Transform hearts and minds! Make this husband NEW! Make this wife NEW! Create a brand-new marriage here - for their good and for Your Glory! Let it be so, in Jesus' Mighty Name!

Your Turn:

1. Separately, take some time to reflect on your personal experience of reading this book. Write down five specific things you are grateful for as a result of this process. At another time, once you are each feeling present, able to act like yourself, and with your Relational Circuits (RC's) on, openly share these gratitude statements with your spouse.

2. Take turns praying for one another out loud, bringing your spouse as well as your marriage before the Father. Ask Him to *transform* you, make you and your spouse *new*, and create a brand-new marriage as you grow closer to Him and each other through Spiritual Intimacy.

3. Set aside time to get quiet before the Lord and ask Jesus, "What invitation are You extending to each of us and to our marriage? How are You calling us deeper in our walk with You and in our relationship?" Now, are you ready to experience *How a YES to God's Invitation Can Transform Your Marriage?*

GLORY FROM THE ASHES

ACKNOWLEDGEMENTS

With deepest gratitude, we thank our loving Heavenly Father, Jesus our Savior and friend, and Holy Spirit our comforter. Thank you for writing our story before even one moment of it unfolded. We treasure Your goodness, and we long to reflect Your glory! Thank you, thank you, thank you.

We are especially grateful to our therapists, Kyle and Monica. You kindly accompanied the two of us toward "Ground Zero" and helped us sort through the rubble as we healed. Thank you for being sensitive to Holy Spirit and guiding us with true wisdom. We can't thank you enough.

We'd also like to thank those who held our story with such grace in the very beginning - you know who you are. Your love, support, encouragement, and acceptance will forever be a priceless treasure to us. Each of you played a part to help bear our burdens, and you displayed such strength as you offered tenderness to our weakness. We are exceedingly grateful for each of you, and we love you dearly.

I (Clinton) want to thank the guys in my Pure Desire group. You were mighty men of valor to me in a time when I was coming undone. I am grateful for your love and acceptance and for joining me in this journey. I will always value your support and friendship.

I also want to thank Pete, who displayed the graciousness of my Heavenly Father in how he held my story. He loved me unconditionally for who I am in Christ and easily saw past my great shortcomings. Pete left this earth on December 6, 2024, and I will miss him fiercely.

I (Nikki) want to thank my Women's Identity Group. At just the right moment, God brought each of you into my life. He knew I would need your love and support, before I had a clue what was coming. God wove my heart together with each of yours, and I'm so grateful! I love you ladies, and I will forever treasure your friendship.

And Amy, what can I say? You understand my heart like few others. How kind of our Father to knit us together when He did. You have been a safe place for me to land, process, and grow, and I greatly appreciate your mutual openness and vulnerability. I love you, Girl!

I want to thank our tribe of pre-readers. Your detailed eyes offering edits and suggestions for clarity in communicating this story were invaluable. The two of us are so thankful for your kind assistance and encouragement along the way.

And last, but not least, a huge THANK YOU to my Sarah-girl. Your many creative talents shine as this book becomes a reality. I'm so thankful for your help formatting our text, designing the cover and other visuals, capturing our *new* wedding photos, and assisting with the logo and website of *Do With Not For Ministries*. But more than your talents, I'm grateful for you – my daughter and friend.

NOTES

Chapter One: Ground Zero

1. "Ground Zero," Oxford Languages Online Dictionary, accessed November 5, 2024, https://www.oed.com/search/dictionary/?scope=Entries&q=ground+zero.
2. Winans, C. (2021). "Goodness of God". On *Believe For It*. Puresprings Gospel Fair Trade Services.

Chapter Three: Is Ignorance Really Bliss?

1. "Ignorance," Britannica Online Dictionary, accessed November 17, 2024, https://www.britannica.com/dictionary/ignorance

Chapter Six: New Take on an Old Problem

1. *Pure Desire Ministries* helps both men and women who are stuck in patterns of unwanted sexual behavior and supports those who've experienced betrayal trauma as a result of others' behaviors. (Discover more at https://puredesire.org/)
2. "Betrayal and Beyond" is a women's support group through *Pure Desire Ministries*.

Chapter Seven: Lightening the Load

1. Maher, M., & Carnes, C. (2020). "Run to the Father". On *Alive and Breathing*. Provident Label Group LLC.
2. Wilder, J., Hendricks, M., & Conover, B. (2020). *The Other Half of Church: Christian Community, Brain Science, and Overcoming Spiritual Stagnation*. Moody Publishers.
3. Hardin, B. (2024). *Daily Audio Bible* (Version 1.3.10) [Mobile App]. App Store.
4. Ephesians 5:25-27 "Husbands, love your wives, just as Christ loved the church and gave himself up for her to make her holy, cleansing her by the washing with water through the word, and to present her to himself as a radiant church, without stain or wrinkle or any other blemish, but holy and blameless."
5. The exercise on the 10 most difficult life events can be found in Roberts, T., & Flanagan, H. (2009). *Seven Pillars of Freedom* (5th ed., pp. 92-99). Pure Desire Ministries International.
6. Stumbo, N., & Windsor, T. (Hosts). (2024, March 5). 7 Lies That Will Ruin Your Life w/Joshua Broome (No. 348) [Audio Podcast Episode]. In *Pure Desire Podcast*.
7. Sharing Joy and Returning to Joy are concepts found in Coursey, C. (2016). *Transforming Fellowship: 19 Brain Skills That Build Joyful Community*. THRIVEtoday.

Chapter Eight: His Ways are Higher

1. Galatians 6:2 "Bear one another's burdens, and so fulfill the law of Christ."
2. Showing tenderness toward someone's weakness is a concept from Wilder, J., Khouri, E., Coursey, C., & Sutton, S. (2013). *Joy Starts Here: The Transformation Zone*. Joy Starts Here Publishers.

Chapter Nine: Ground Zero - The Other Side of the Coin

1. John 14:6 "Jesus said to him, "I am the way, and the truth, and the life. No one comes to the Father except through me."
2. 1 Corinthians 6:19-20 "Or do you not know that your body is a temple of the Holy Spirit within you, whom you have received from God? You are not your own, for you were bought with a great price. So glorify God in your body."
3. Winans, C. (2021). "Goodness of God". On *Believe For It*. Puresprings Gospel Fair Trade Services.
4. Jenkins, D. (2017-2024). *The Chosen* [TV series]. 5&2 Studios.
5. Ransomed Heart. (2024). *One Minute Pause* (Version 12.2.0) [Mobile App]. App Store.

Chapter Ten: Healing Begins

1. Gray, J. (2011). "Nothing is Wasted". On *A Way to See in the Dark*. Centricity Music.
2. Fretwell, P., & Fretwell, P. (Hosts). (2022, February 8). How to be HOT Every Day (Honest, Open, and Transparent (No. 4). [Audio Podcast Episode]. In *Savage Marriage Ministries with Phil & Priscilla*.
3. Coursey, C. (2021). *The Joy Switch: How Your Brain's Secret Circuit Affects Your Relationships-And How You Can Activate It.* Northfield Publishing. Concepts on Relational Circuits also taken from Lehman, K. (2011). *Outsmarting Yourself: Catching Your Past Invading the Present and What to Do About It.* This JOY! Books.
4. Warner, M., & Coursey, C. (2019). *The 4 Habits of Joy-Filled Marriages: How 15 Minutes a Day Will Help You Stay in Love.* Northfield Publishing.
5. Penner, C. & Penner, J. (1993). *Restoring the Pleasure: Complete Step-By-Step Program to Help Couples Overcome the Most Common Sexual Barriers* (pp. 14-15). W Publishing Group.

Chapter Eleven: Stepping Toward Forgiveness

1. Coursey, C. (2016). *Transforming Fellowship: 19 Brains Skills That Build Joyful Community.* THRIVEtoday.
2. Wilder, J., Hendricks, M., & Conover, B. (2020). *The Other Half of Church: Christian Community, Brain Science, and Overcoming Spiritual Stagnation* (p.54). Moody Publishers.

Chapter Twelve: Moving at Warp Speed

1. Ransomed Heart. (2024). *One Minute Pause* (Version 12.2.0) [Mobile App]. App Store.
2. Wilder, J., Kang, A., Loppnow, J., & Loppnow, S. (2015). *Joyful Journey: Listening to Immanuel.* Presence and Practice.
3. Wilder, J., Kang, A., Loppnow, J., & Loppnow, S. (2015). *Joyful Journey: Listening to Immanuel* (p. 17). Presence and Practice.
4. The background instrumental music for the "One Minute Pause" app provided by Augusto, W. (2019). *Soaking in His Presence, Volume 3.* In His Presence.

Chapter Fourteen: A Trip of a Lifetime

1. Pierpoint, F. (1864). *For the Beauty of the Earth.* Public Domain.
2. Bercaw, B. & Bercaw, G. (2010). *The Couple's Guide to Intimacy: How Sexual Reintegration Therapy Can Help Your Relationship Heal.* CreateSpace.
3. The "30 Days to Resilient" program can be found on Ransomed Heart. (2024). *One Minute Pause* (Version 12.2.0) [Mobile App]. App Store.

Chapter Fifteen: Intimacy - Let's Get Down to Business

1. "Act Like Myself" is Skill 12 found in Coursey, C. (2016). *Transforming Fellowship: 19 Brains Skills That Build Joyful Community* (pp. 169-178). THRIVEtoday.
2. Explanation of the acronym C.A.K.E. can be found in Warner, M., & Coursey, C. (2019). *The 4 Habits of Joy-Filled Marriages: How 15 Minutes a Day Will Help You Stay in Love* (pp. 27-40). Northfield Publishing.

Chapter Seventeen: Living in the Light

1. Peacock, C. (1991). "In the Light". On *Love Life*. Sparrow Records.
2. James 5:16 "Therefore, confess your sins to one another and pray for one another, that you may be healed. The prayer of a righteous person has great power as it is working."
3. Confessional Community is not a new concept, but you can find valuable information in the entire Season 7 of Dr. Curt Thompson's "Being Known Podcast" found in Thompson, C., & Sweeney, P. (Hosts). (2021-present). *Being Known Podcast*. [Audio Podcast].

If you've been blessed by our story and want to learn more about the hope we're sharing with other couples, check out our non-profit *Do With Not For Ministries*.

DWN4.org

We'd love to hear from you! Email us at info@DWN4.org to connect!

THRIVEtoday
relational living in practice

Relational skills are brain-based skills that give us the ability and capacity to build meaningful connections with the people in our lives. With practice, relational skills are what we use to maintain our relationships during strain, conflicts and difficulties so we endure hardship well as we stay connected.

Learn More with one of our introductory resources:

The Joy Switch Book - Discover how your brain's secret circuit affects your relationships and how you can activate it.

The Foundational 5 Introductory Course - Explore and practice the Foundational 5 relational skills.

Relational Skills in Real Life Podcast - Be inspired through 10-15 minute episodes featuring stories of how relational skills are impacting lives.

www.thrivetoday.org
info@thrivetoday.org

SAVAGE
MARRIAGE MINISTRIES

Savage Marriage equips couples to overcome wounds of the past to find forgiveness, experience freedom, and embrace hope for the future.

SavageMarriageMinistries.com

Check out our podcast: *Savage Marriage Ministries with Phil & Pricilla* on your favorite platform.

Find our award-winning book and study guide on Amazon!

CENTER FOR TRANSFORMATION

THE INSTITUTE

Visit the CFT Institute for Therapists

www.cftinstitute.com

THE PRACTICE

Learn more abouut our LMIT Practice right here in NC

www.familytransformation.com

The Center for Transformation Institute was founded in 2022 by a group of therapists who have implemented a model that has helped them grow personally in ways that directly apply to their work with clients. CFT Institute is currently partnering with Life Model Works to bring this model (the Life Model) to therapists everywhere! This therapist team has not only learned and applied the Life Model personally, but they are also working diligently to offer therapists the best resources to learn and apply the Life Model personally and professionally. We believe the Life Model is the solution to your frustrations because it gives the knowledge and skill to live out your personal healing and become your professional best!

The Center for Family Transformation exists in the Lake Norman area of Charlotte, NC, and specializes in therapeutic intervention, prevention and treatment for adolescents, young adults and their families. The goal is to restore healthy identity in each individual and to renew connection and belonging to the family. Our hope is that this will prevent mental health struggles, traumatic experiences and addiction issues from stealing the future of the clients and families we serve.

If you'd like to learn more, email us at:
info@familytransformation.com

The Pause App

Take a pause.

A simple way to connect with God in the middle of your busy day.

From John Eldredge, the New York Times Best-Selling Author of *Wild at Heart* and *Captivating*.

Based on the "One Minute Pause" chapter of his new books *Get Your Life Back* and *Resilient*, this app invites you into the simple practice of releasing everything to God, restoring your union with God, and inviting Him to fill you.

Made in the USA
Columbia, SC
06 April 2025